The True Life Story of Swiftwater Bill Gates

The True
Life Story of
Swiftwater Bill Gates

**By His
Mother-in-Law,
Mrs. Iola Bebbe.**

TABLE OF CONTENTS.

PREFACE.

I T may seem odd to Alaskans, and by that I mean, the men and women who really live in the remote, yet near, northern gold country, that "Swiftwater Bill"— known to both the old Sour Doughs and the Cheechacos—should have asked me to write the real story of his life, yet this is really the fact.

Bill Gates is in some ways, and indeed in many, one of the most remarkable men that the lust for gold ever produced in any clime or latitude.

Remarkable?

Yes—that's the word—and possibly nothing more remarkable than that he, in a confiding moment said to me as he held his first born child in his arms in the little cabin on Quartz Creek, in the Klondike, where he had amassed and spent a fortune of $500,-000:

"I'd like somebody to write my life story. Will you do it?"

I can only believe that the romantic element in Swift Water Bill's character—a character as changeful and variegated as the kaleidoscope—led Swiftwater Bill to ask me to do him this service. I was then the mother of his wife—the grandmother of his child. The sacredness of the relation must be apparent.

Probably a great many people—hundreds, perhaps—may say that my labor is one that can have no reward, and these may speak ill things of Swiftwater, saying, perhaps, that he is more inclined to do royally by strangers and to forget those who have aided and befriended him.

I am not to judge Swiftwater Bill, nor do I wish him to be judged except as the individual reader of this little work may wish so to do.

If he has turned against those near and dear to him—if he has preferred to give prodigally of gold to strangers, while at the same time forgetting his own obligations—I am not the one to point the finger of rebuke at his eccentricities.

For this reason, the narrative within these covers is confined to the facts relating to the career of Swiftwater Bill—a character worthy of the pen of a Dickens or a Dumas—with his faults and his virtues impartially portrayed as best I can do.

IOLA BEEBE,

Mother-in-law of Swiftwater Bill.

MRS. IOLA BEEBE,
Mother-in-law of Swiftwater Bill.

CHAPTER I.

LITTLE, low-eaved, common, ordinary looking road house, built of logs, with one room for the bunks, another for a kitchen and a third for miscellaneous purposes, used to be well known to travelers in the Yukon Valley in Alaska at Circle City. The straggling little mining camp, its population divided between American, French-Canadians of uncertain pedigree, and Indians with an occasional admixture of canny Scotchmen, whose conversation savored strongly of the old Hudson Bay Trading Company's days in the far north, enjoyed no reputation outside of Forty Mile, Juneau and the Puget Sound cities of Seattle and Tacoma. From the wharves of these cities in 1895 there left at infrequent intervals, small chuggy, wobbly steamers for Southeastern Alaska points usually carrying in the spring months motley cargoes of yelping dogs, rough coated, bearded, tanned miners and prospectors from all points of the globe, and great quantities of canned goods of every description.

In those days the eager and hardy prospector who fared forth to the Yukon's dangers in search of gold was usually indifferent to whatever fate befell him. He figured that at best the odds were over-

whelmingly against him, with just one chance, or
maybe ten, in a hundred of striking a pay streak. It
was inevitable that a great proportion of the ven-
turous and ignorant Chechacos, or newcomers, who
paid their dollars by the hundred to the steamship
companies in Seattle, should, after failing in the
search for gold, seek means of gaining a miserable .
existence in some wage paid vocation.

Were it in my power to bring my hero on the
stage under more auspicious circumstances than
those of which I am about to tell, I would gladly
do it. But the truth must be told of Swiftwater
Bill, and at the time of the opening of my narrative
—and this was before the world had ever heard the
least hint of the wonderful Klondike gold discovery
—Swiftwater stood washing dishes in the kitchen of
the road-house I have just described.

The place was no different from any one of a
thousand of these little log shelters where men, traveling back and forth in the dead of winter with dog
teams, find temporary lodging and a hurried meal of
bacon and beans and canned stuff. It was broad day-
light, although the clock showed eleven P. M., in
August, 1896. The sun scarcely seemed to linger
more than an hour beneath the horizon at nightfall,
to re-appear a shimmering ball of light at three
o'clock in the morning.

"Bring us another pot of coffee!" shouted one

of three prospectors, who sat with their elbows on the table, greedily licking up the remnants of a huge platter full of bacon and beans garnished with some strips of cold, canned roast beef and some evaporated potatoes, which had been made into a kind of stew.

The hero of my sketch wiped his hands on a greasy towel and, taking a dirty, black tin coffee pot from the top of the Yukon stove, he hurried in to serve his customers.

One of these was six feet two, broad-shouldered, sparsely built, hatchet faced, with a long nose, keen blue eyes and with auburn colored hair falling almost to his shoulders. French Joe was the name he went by, and no more intrepid trapper and prospector ever lived in the frozen valley of the Yukon than he. The other two were nondescripts—one with a coarse yellow jumper, the other in a dark blue suit of cast off army clothes. The man in the jumper was bearded, short and chunky, of German extraction, while the other was a half-blood Indian.

Swiftwater, as he ambled into the room, one hand holding his dirty apron, the other holding the coffee pot, was not such a man as to excite the interest of even a wayfarer in the road-house at Circle. About 35 years old, five feet five inches tall, a scraggly growth of black whiskers on his chin, and long, wavy moustaches of the same color, curling from his

HASH $4.00
BUNKS $5.00
TERMS CASH.

SWIFTWATER HEARS FROM FRENCH JOE THE FIRST
NEWS OF THE GOLD DISCOVERY IN THE KLONDIKE.

upper lip, Swiftwater did not arouse even a passing
glance from the trio at the table.

"Boys, de' done struck it, al' right, 'cause Indian
George say it's all gold from ze gras' roots, on Bonanza. An' it's only a leetle more'n two days polin'
up ze river from ze T'hoandike.''

It was French Joe who spoke, and then when
he drew forth a little bottle containing a few ounces
of gold nuggets and dust, Swiftwater Bill, as he
poured the third cup of coffee, gazed open mouthed
on the showing of yellow treasure.

It is only necessary to say that from that moment
Swiftwater was attentive to the needs of his three
guests, and when he had overheard all of their talk
he silently, but none the less positively, made up
his mind to quit his job forthwith and to "mush"
for the new gold fields.

And this is why it was that, the next morning, the
little Circle City road-house was minus a dishwasher
and all round handyman. And before the little com-
munity was well astir, far in the distance, up the
Yukon river, might have been seen the little, dark
bearded man poling for dear life in a flat-bottom
boat, whose prow was pointed in the direction of the
Klondike river.

CHAPTER II.

I T WOULD be useless to encumber my story with a lengthy and detailed narrative of Swiftwater Bill's experiences in the first mad rush of gold-seekers up the narrow and devious channels of Bonanza and Eldorado Creeks. The world has for eleven years known the entrancing story of George Carmack's find on Bonanza—how, from the first spadeful of grass roots, studded with gold dust and nuggets, which filled a tiny vial, the gravel beds

of Bonanza and Eldorado and a few adjoining creeks, all situated within the area of a township or two, produced the marvelous sum of $50,000,000 within a few years.

Swiftwater struck gold from the very first. He located No. 13 Eldorado, and had as his neighbors such well known mining men as Prof. T. S. Lippy, the Seattle millionaire, who left a poorly paid job as physical director of the Y. M. C. A. in Seattle to prospect for gold in Alaska; Ole Oleson; the Berry Bros., who cleaned up a million dollars on two and a fraction claims on Eldorado; Antone Stander; Michael Dore, a young French-Canadian, who died from exposure in a little cabin surrounded by tin oil cans filled to overflowing with the yellow metal, and others equally well known.

Swiftwater's ground on No. 13 Eldorado was fabulously rich—so rich that after he had struck the pay streak, the excitement was too much for him and he forthwith struck out for the trail that leads to Dawson. And now I am about to reveal to Alaskans and others who read this little book a quality about Swiftwater of which few people had any knowledge whatever, and this shows in a startling way how easy it was in those halcyon days in the Golden Klondike' for a man to grasp a fortune of a million dollars in an instant and then throw it away with the ease and indifference that a smoker discards a half-burned cigar.

Swiftwater, as may well be imagined, when he struck the rich layers of gold in the candle-lit crevices of bedrock on Eldorado a few feet below the surface, could have had a half interest in a half dozen claims on each side of him if he had simply kept his mouth shut and informed those he knew in Dawson of the strike, on condition that they would share half and half with him. This was a common transaction in those days and a perfectly legitimate one, and Swiftwater could have cleaned up that winter beyond question $1,000,000 in gold dust, after paying all expenses and doing very little work himself, had he exercised the most common, ordinary business ability.

Instead, Swiftwater, when he struck Dawson, threw down a big poke of gold on the bar of a saloon and announced his intention of buying out the finest gambling hall and bar in town. Dawson was then the roughest kind of a frontier mining camp, although the mounted police preserved very good order. There were at least a score of gambling halls in Dawson and as many more dance halls. The gambling games ran continually twenty-four hours a day, and the smallest wager usually made, even in the poorest games, was an ounce of gold, or almost $20.

When Bill laid down his poke of gold on the bar of a Dawson saloon—it was so heavy he could hardly lift it—he was instantly surrounded by a mob of thirty or forty men and a few women.

"Why, boys!" said Swiftwater, ordering a case of wine for the thirsty, while he chose appolinaris himself, "that's easy enough! All you've got to do is to go up to Eldorado Creek and you can get all the gold you want by simply working a rocker about a week."

That settled the fate of Eldorado, for the next day before three o'clock in the morning there was a stampede to the new find, and in twenty-four hours the whole creek had been staked from mouth to source.

Comfortably enjoying the knowledge that he had $300,000 or $400,000 in gold to the good, Swiftwater set about finding ways to spend it.

His first order "to the outside" was for a black Prince Albert coat and a black silk top hat, which came in in about five or six weeks and were immediately donned by Swiftwater. By this time he had become the owner of the Monte Carlo, the biggest gambling hall in Dawson.

"Tear the roof off, boys!" Swiftwater said when the players on the opening night swarmed in and asked what was the limit of the bets.

"The sky is the limit and raise her up as far as

you want to go, boys,'' said Swiftwater, ''and if the
roof's in your way, tear it off!''

Just about this time came the first of Swiftwater's
affaires d' l'amour, because a day or two previously
five young women of the Juneau dance halls had
floated down the river in a barge and gone to work
in Dawson. There were two sisters in the group.
Both of them were beautiful women, young, bright,
entertaining and clever in the way such women are.
They were Gussie and May Lamore.

''I am going to have a lady and the swellest that's
in the country,'' Swiftwater told his friends, and
then, donning his best clothes, the costliest he could
buy in Dawson, Swiftwater went over to the dance
hall, where the Lamore sisters were working, and
ordered wine for everybody on the floor.

Gussie was dancing with a big, brawny, French-
Canadian miner. Her little feet seemed scarcely to
touch the floor of the dance hall as the miner
whirled her around and around. She was little,
plump, beautifully formed and with a face of more
than passing comeliness.

You women of ''the States''—when I say ''the
States'' I simply speak of our country as do all the
old-timers in Alaska, and not as if it was some
foreign country, but as it really is to us, the home
of ourselves and our forebears, yet separated from
us by thousands of miles of iceclad mountain barriers

and storm swept seas have no conception of the dance hall girl as a type of the early days of Dawson. Many of the were of good families, young, comely, and fairly well educated. What stress or storm befell them, or other inhospitable element in their lives drove them to the northern gold mining country, God knows it is not my portion to tell. Nor could any one of them probably, in telling her own life story, give the reasons for the appearance in these dance halls of any of her sisters.

It is enough for you and me to understand—and it requires no unusual insight into the human heart and its mysteries to do so—that when a miner had spent a few months in the solitude of the hills and gold lined gulches of the Yukon Valley, if he finally found the precious gold on the rim of the bedrock, his first thought was to go back to "town."

Back to town? Yes, because "town" meant and still means to those hardy men any place where human beings are assembled, and the dance hall, in those rough days, was the center of social activities and gaieties.

The sight of little Gussie Lamore, with her skirt just touching the tops of her shoes, spinning around in a waltz with that big French-Canadian, set all of Bill's amorous nature aglow. He went to the hotel, filled his pockets with pokes of gold dust and came quickly back to the dance hall, where he obtained an introduction to Gussie.

Bill's wooing was of the rapid kind. Before the night was over he had told Gussie—

"I'll give you your weight in gold tomorrow morning if you will marry me—and I guess you'll weigh about $30,000."

Pretty Gussie shook her head coquettishly. "We will just be friends, Swiftwater, and I guess that'll be about all."

Of course, it was only a day or two before all Dawson knew of Swiftwater's infatuation. The two became fast friends and got along beautifully for a week or two. Then came a bitter quarrel, and from that arose the incident which gave Swiftwater Bill almost his greatest fame—it is the story of how he cornered the egg market in Dawson in a valiant effort to hold the love of his sweetheart, Gussie Lamore.

It was in the spring of 1898 and Dawson was very short of grub of every kind. The average meal of canned soup, a plate of beans garnished by a few slices of bacon or canned meat, with a little side dish of canned or dried potatoes stewed, hot cakes or biscuit and coffee, cost about $5 and sometimes more. The cheapest meal for two persons was $10, and Bill had seen to it, while trying to win Gussie for his wife, that she had the best there was to eat in Dawson.

The two were inseparable on the streets. Then came the quarrel—it was simply a little lovers' dispute, and then the break.

Swiftwater put in two days assiduously cultivating the friendly graces of the other dance hall girls in Dawson, but Gussie cared not.

One night an adventurous trader came down from the Upper Yukon in a small boat—there were no steamers then—and brought two crates of fresh eggs from Seattle.

Swiftwater heard of this, and he knew that there would be a tremendous demand for those eggs, as the miners usually made their breakfasts of the evaporated article; so, shrewdly, he went immediately to the restaurant which had purchased the crates and called for the proprietor.

Now, this worthy knew Swiftwater to be immensely wealthy and a very good customer, so when the Eldorado miner demanded the right to buy every egg in the house, which meant every egg in town, the restaurant man stroked his chin and said:

"Swiftwater, those eggs cost me a big lot of money, and there hain't no more. You can have the hull outfit for three dollars an egg, in dust."

There was just one whole crate left, and Swiftwater weighed out $2,280 in gold dust.

"Those eggs are mine—keep them here and don't let anybody have any."

Now, Swiftwater and Gussie had been in the habit of breakfasting on fresh eggs some days before, when the first infrequent trader of the season had managed, after enduring several wrecks on the upper river, to reach Dawson. Fresh eggs were to Gussie what chocolates and bon bons are to the average girl in the States.

The next morning Swiftwater arrived at the restaurant for breakfast, a little earlier than usual, and in a few minutes the waiter placed before him a steaming hot platter containing an even dozen of the eggs, nicely poached and served on small strips of toast.

Just then Gussie came in for her breakfast and seated herself at the other end of the little dining room. It was long after the usual hour for breakfast, and they were the only two in the room. Without doing Swiftwater the honor of passing so much as a glance in his direction, Gussie said to the waiter:

"Bring me a full order of fried eggs."

"We ain't got no eggs, mum; they was all sold out last night," said the waiter.

Gussie's face flamed with anger, but only for an instant. Then she picked up her plate, her knife

SWIFTWATER AND GUSSIE LAMORE ARE RECONCILED
OVER A HOT PLATTER OF FRESH EGGS, AT DAWSON.

and fork and napkin and strode over to the table where Swiftwater sat.

"I guess I'll have some eggs, after all," said Gussie, without looking at Swiftwater, as she liberally helped herself from his platter.

Then both of them burst out laughing and peace reigned once more between them.

Of course, Swiftwater figured that he had won a substantial victory by reaching Gussie's heart through her stomach. But, as a matter of fact, we all figured that the laugh was on Swiftwater, and I think every woman who reads this story will agree with me.

CHAPTER III.

SWIFTWATER has often told me that he never could quite understand why it was that the way to a woman's heart, even his own way—Swiftwater's—was so hard to travel and so devious and tortuous in its windings and interwindings.

"Why, Mrs. Beebe," Swiftwater used to say, "I should think a man could do anything with gold! And for my own part, I used to always figure that money would buy anything," said Swiftwater, "even the most beautiful woman in the world for your wife."

Swiftwater's mental processes were simple, as the foregoing will illustrate. It was hardly to be expected otherwise. Swiftwater decamped from the drudgery and slavish toil of a kitchen in the little road-house at Circle City to gain in less than three months more money than he had ever dreamed it possible for him to have.

Two hundred thousand dollars was the minimum of Swiftwater's first big cleanup. If Gussie Lamore had lovers, Swiftwater figured, his money would win her heart away from all the rest.

.All this relates very intimately to the really

interesting story of Swiftwater's courtship of Gussie
Lamore. The girl kept him at arm's length, yet if
ever Swiftwater became restive Gussie would
cleverly draw the line taut and Swiftwater was at
her feet.

"I am tired of this, Gussie," said Swiftwater
one day, and finally the "Knight of the Golden
Omelette," as he was often termed, was serious for
once in his life.

"I am going back to Eldorado and I'll bring
down here a bunch of gold. It will weigh as much
as you do on the scales, pound for pound. Gussie,
that gold will be yours if you give me your word
you will marry me."

"All right, Bill, we'll see. Go get your gold and
show me that you really have it."

Swiftwater was gone from Dawson about two
days before he returned to the dance hall where
Gussie was working. This time he kept away from
the bar and merely waited until the morning
dawned and the habitues of the dance hall had dis-
appeared one by one. By that time the word had
been sent out to Seattle of the rich findings of gold
on Eldorado, and the early crop of newcomers was
arriving over the ice from Dyea, in the days before
the Skagway trail was known.

Swiftwater, in the early morning, carried to Gussie's apartments two tin coffee cans filled with the yellow gold.

"Here's all you weigh, anyhow," said Swiftwater. "Now, take this gold to the Trading Company's office and bank it. Then I want you to buy a ticket to San Francisco and I will meet you there this summer and we will be married."

Thus ended the curious story of Swiftwater's wooing of Gussie Lamore. All the world knows how, when Gussie reached San Francisco, where her folks lived, she banked Swiftwater's gold and turned him down cold.

Swiftwater reached the Golden Gate a month after Gussie had arrived at her home. All his entreaties for her to carry out her bargain came to nothing.

Bitter as he was towards Gussie, Swiftwater still seemed to love the girl. His first creed, "I can buy any woman with gold," seemed to stick with him.

There was, for one thing, little Grace Lamore. It came to Swiftwater that he could marry Grace and punish Gussie for her inconstancy.

Now, this may seem to you, my reader, like an ill-founded story. Yet the truth is, Grace and Swiftwater were married within a month of his arrival in San Francisco, and the San Francisco papers were filled with the story of how Swiftwater bought his bride a $15,000 home in Oakland and furnished it most beautifully with all that money could buy.

Swiftwater and Grace, after a two days' wedding trip down the San Joaquin Valley leased the bridal chamber of the Baldwin Hotel, while their new home in Oakland was being fitted up. Old-time Alaskans will smile when I recall the impression that Swiftwater made on San Franciscans.

It was his invariable custom to stand in front of the lobby of the Baldwin every evening, smoothly shaved, his moustaches nicely brushed and curled, and wearing his favorite black Prince Albert and silk hat.

Probably few in the throng that came and went through the lobby of the Baldwin—in those days one of the most popular hostelries in San Francisco —would have paid any attention to Swiftwater. But Bill knew a trick or two and his old-time friends have told me that Swiftwater made it an unfailing custom to tip the bell-boys a dollar each a day to point to the dapper little man and have them tell both guests of the Baldwin and strangers:

"There is Swiftwater Bill Gates, the King of the Klondike."

And Swiftwater would stand every evening, silk hat on his head, spick and span, and clean, and bow politely to everybody as they came in through the lobby to the dining hall.

SWIFTWATER GREETS STRANGERS IN THE LOBBY OF
THE BALDWIN HOTEL, WHOM HE HAD NEVER SEEN
BEFORE.

Isn't it curious, that with all his money, and his confidence in the purchasing power of gold, Swiftwater's dream of love with Grace Lamore should have lasted scarcely more than a short three weeks? It was not that Swiftwater was parsimonious with is money—the very finest of silks and satins, millinery, diamonds at Shreve's, cut glass and silverware, were Grace's for the asking. They will tell you in San Francisco to this day that Swiftwater and his bride worked overtime in a carriage shopping in the most expensive houses in the city of the Golden Gate.

Then came the break with Grace. I do not know the cause, but the girl threw Swiftwater overboard and left the bridal chamber of the Baldwin to return to her family, even before they had occupied the palatial home in Oakland.

Swiftwater's rage knew no bounds. In his heart he cursed the whole Lamore family and quickly took means to vent his spite.

This is how it came about that scarcely a month after Swiftwater's wedding bells had rung, the "Knight of the Golden Omelette" was seen to enter his Oakland home one evening and emerge therefrom a half hour later bearing on his back a heavy bundle wrapped in a bed sheet.

The burden was all that Swiftwater's strength could manage. Laboriously he toiled his way to

SWIFTWATER BILL CARRYING $7,000 WORTH OF WED-
DING PRESENTS FROM HIS BRIDE'S HOME IN OAK-
LAND.

the house of a friend in Oakland and wearily deposited his bundle on the front porch, where he sat and waited the coming of his friend.

When Swiftwater was finally admitted to the house, he untied the sheet and opened up the contents of the pack. There lay glittering on the floor $7,000 worth of solid silver plate and cut glass.

"That's what I gave my bride," he said, "and now she's quit me and I'm d——d if she'll have that."

CHAPTER IV.

IT HAS always seemed a standing wonder to me that when Swiftwater had separated himself from about $100,000 or more in gold dust with the Lamore sisters as the chief beneficiaries, and after he had been divorced from Grace, following her refusal to live with him in San Francisco, he did not finally come within a rifle shot of the realization of the real value of money. There is no doubt but that Swiftwater was bitterly resentful towards Gussie and Grace Lamore after they had both thrown him overboard, and you will no doubt agree with me that to an ordinary man such experiences as these would have had a sobering effect.

Instead, however, the miner plunged more recklessly than ever into all manner of money-making and money-spending, and the only reason that Swiftwater Bill Gates is not ranked today with Flood, Mackay and Fair as one of a group of the greatest and richest mining men the Pacific Coast has produced, is that he did not have the balance wheel of caution and discretion that is given to the ordinary artisan or day laborer.

Swiftwater left San Francisco soon after his rupture with Grace Lamore and went directly to Ottawa, Canada, where, marvelous as it may seem in the light of the ten years of mining history in the north, Swiftwater induced the Dominion government to grant him a concession on Quartz Creek, in the Klondike, worth today millions upon millions.

This concession covered an immense tract of ground at least three miles long and in some places two miles wide. Much of the ground was very rich, and today, ten years later, it is paying big dividends. Yet rich as it was and immensely valuable as was the enormous concession, Swiftwater induced the Dominion of Canada authorities to part with it for merely a nominal consideration. His success in this respect cannot be otherwise regarded than phenomenal. Although his money was nearly all gone, Swiftwater, taking a new grip on himself, and entirely disregardful of the fates which had been so lavish to him, went from Ottawa to London, England, where he obtained enough money to buy and ship to Dawson one of the largest and most expensive hydraulic plants in the country.

When this plant was shipped to Seattle in 1898, Swiftwater followed it to the city on Elliott Bay.

It was the day following Swiftwater Bill's arrival in Seattle from San Francisco in the spring of 1899 that Mr. Richardson, an old Seattle friend of mine, who knew Gates well, telephoned me that

Swiftwater had an elegant suite of apartments at the Butler Hotel, and that he had asked him to arrange for an introduction. Mr. Richardson said over the telephone:

"You ought to know Swiftwater—he knows everybody in Dawson and the Klondike, and for a woman like you to go into that country with a big hotel outfit and no friends would be ridiculous."

When I think of what happened to me and my daughters, Blanche and Bera, in the next few days following this incident, and of the years of wretchedness and misery and laying waste of human lives and happiness that came after, I am tempted to wonder what curious form of an unseen fate shapes our destinies and turns and twists our fortunes in all manner of devious and uncertain ways.

My whole hotel outfit had gone up to St. Michael the fall previous and I with it—and at great cost of labor and trouble I had seen to it, at St. Michael, that the precious shipment—representing all I had in the world—was safely stored aboard a river steamer bound for Dawson.

Now, spring had come again, and with it the big rush to the gold fields of the Yukon was on, and Seattle was again filled with a seething, surging, struggling, discontented, optimistic, laughing crowd of gold hunters of every nationality and color.

It was almost worth your life to try to break through the mob and gain admission to the lobby of the Hotel Butler in those days, for the place was absolutely packed at night with men as thick as sardines in a box, and all shouting and gesticulating and keeping up such a clatter that it drove one nearly crazy.

It was no place for a woman, and the few women whose fortunes or whose husbands had brought them thither were seated in a little parlor on the second floor, where they could easily hear the clamor and confusion that came from the noisy mob in the lobby.

In the crowd were such old-time sourdoughs as Ole Olson, who sold out a little piece of ground about as big as a city block on Eldorado for $250,-000, after he had taken out as much more in three months' work the winter previous; "French Curley" De Lorge, known from White Horse to the mouth of the Tanana as one of the Yukon's bravest and strongest hearted trappers and freighters; Joe Ladue, who laid out the town of Dawson; George Carmack, whose Indian brother-in-law, Skookum Jim, is supposed to have turned over the first spadeful of grass roots studded with gold on the banks of Bonanza; big Tom Henderson, who found gold before anybody, he always said, on Quartz Creek; Joe Ward-

ner and Phil O'Rourke, both famous in the Coeur
d'Alenes; Henry Bratnober, six feet two, black
beard, shaggy black hair and black eyes, over-
bearing and coarse voiced, the representative in
the golden north of the Rothschilds of London; and
men almost equally well known from Australia,
from South Africa and from continental Europe,
including the vigilant and energetic Count Carbon-
neau of Paris.

By appointment, Swiftwater, attired in immacu-
late black broadcloth Prince Albert, low cut vest,
patent leather shoes, shimmering "biled" shirt,
with a four-karat diamond gleaming like an electric
light from his bosom, stood waiting for us in the
parlor. I had left Bera, who was fifteen years old,
in my apartments in the Hinckley Block and had
taken Blanche, my eldest daughter, with me.

"I am awfully glad to meet you, Mrs. Beebe,"
said Swiftwater, advancing with step as noiseless as
a Maltese cat, as he walked across the heavy plush
carpet.

Swiftwater put out a soft womanish hand,
grasped mine and spoke in a low musical voice, the
kind of voice that instantly wins the confidence of
nine women out of ten.

"I have heard that you were going in this spring,
and as I know how hard it is for a woman to get
along in that country without someone to befriend

her, I was very glad indeed to have the chance of
extending you all the aid in my power," continued
Swiftwater, in the meantime glancing in an interested way at Blanche, who stood near the piano.

"This is my daughter, Blanche, Mr. Gates," I
said. Blanche was then nineteen years old, and
I had taken her out of the Convent school in Portland to keep me company in the north, along with
Bera.

It only took us a few minutes to agree that when
I arrived in Dawson, if Swiftwater was there first,
he should help me in getting a location for my
hotel and settling down. Then, as I arose to go,
he said, turning again to Blanche:

"Doesn't your daughter play the piano, Mrs.
Beebe? I am very fond of music."

Blanche, at a nod from me, sat down and began
to play some simple little thing, when Swiftwater
said:

"Please excuse me, I have a friend with me."

In a moment Swiftwater returned and in-
troduced his friend, a tall, lithe, clean-cut, smooth
shaven Englishman of about thirty-five—Mr. Hathaway.

Five minutes later, Blanche having pleased both
men with her playing, arose from the piano.

"Now, we are just going down to dinner in the
grill; won't you please join us, ladies?" said Swift-

water in those deliciously velvet tones which seemed
to put any woman at perfect ease in his company.

A shivery feeling came over me, and I said: ''No,
I think we will go right home.''

Now, I never could tell for the life of me just
what made me want to hurry away with my Blanche
from the hotel and Swiftwater Bill. His friend
Hathaway was a nice clean looking sort of a
chap and very gentlemanly, and Swiftwater was
the absolute quintessence of gentlemanly conduct
and chivalry. But the papers had told all about
Swiftwater and Gussie and Grace Lamore—only
that the reporters, as well as the general public,
seemed to regard it all as a joke—Gussie's turning
down Swiftwater after he had given her her weight
in gold—about $30,000 in virgin dust and nuggets—
and then Bill's marrying Grace, her sister, for spite.
The whole yarn struck me so funny, that as we
walked, with difficulty, through the crowds on Second Avenue to our apartments, I could not think of
anything mean or vicious about Swiftwater.

Nevertheless, I scrupulously avoided inviting
Swiftwater to call, and after I had concluded my
business with him, I determined to have nothing
more to do with him until business matters made it
necessary in Dawson. You women, who live ''on
the outside'' and have never been over the trail and
down the Yukon in a scow, can never know what

fortitude is necessary for a woman to cut loose from the States and make her own way in business in a new gold camp like Dawson was in 1899.

So it was only natural, that, knowing Swiftwater to be one of the leading and richest men in that country, I should have accepted his offer of assistance and advice. God only knows how different would have been all our lives could I but have foreseen the awful misery and wretchedness and ruin which that man Swiftwater easily worked in the lives of three innocent people who had never done him wrong, or anyone else, for that matter.

Three days after my glimpse of Swiftwater Bill, Bera and myself were just finishing dressing for dinner in my big sitting room. It was rather warm for a spring evening in Seattle, and we were all hungry. Blanche was waiting near the door fully dressed, I was putting on my gloves, and little Bera, fifteen years old, stood in front of the mirror trying to fasten down a big bunch of wavy brown hair of silken glossy texture, which was doing its best to get from under her big white Leghorn hat, the child looking the very picture of beauty and innocence.

She was plump, with deliciously pink cheeks, great big blue eyes, regular features and she wore a dress I had had made at great expense in Victoria —it was of dark blue voile, close fitting, with a lining of red silk, which showed the cardinal as the girl turned and walked across the room and then back again to the mirror. Her white Leghorn hat was trimmed with large red roses. I heard a noise, as if someone had knocked and Bera, turning quickly, said under her breath, as if alarmed:

"Mama! There is somebody there!"

I looked and there stood Swiftwater, silk hat in hand, smiling, bowing, one foot across the threshold, while behind him loomed the tall form of his friend Hathaway.

"Pardon us, won't you, Mrs. Beebe, but we want you to go to dinner with us at the Butler. Won't you do so and bring the girls?" and Swiftwater instantly turned his eyes from mine and looked at Bera standing in front of the mirror, her face flushed, her eyes sparkling with excitement and her form silhouetted against a red plush curtain which covered the door to the adjoining room.

Before I could gather my wits about me I had accepted Swiftwater's invitation. It was the only thing I could do, because we were just about to go to dinner ourselves, and he seemed to know that instinctively, and that I could not very well refuse.

CHAPTER V.

"MAMA," said Bera to me, "Mrs. Ainslee is not nearly so well today, and Mr. Hathaway said when he came down from the hospital this after- noon that she wanted to see you sure this evening about seven o'clock."

Mrs. Ainslee had been desperately ill at Providence Hospital for weeks and she was a woman of whom I had known in earlier days and whose sad plight—her husband was dead and she was alone in the world—had induced me to do all I could for her.

It was scarcely more than a week following the evening that Swiftwater and Mr. Hathaway was host at dinner at the hotel, that Bera took, what I real- ized afterwards, was an unusual and unexpected in- terest in Mrs. Ainslee's case. Since the dinner engage- ment, Swiftwater had been just ordinarily attentive to myself and my two daughters, although frequent- ly asking us to go to the theatre with him and sending flowers almost daily to our apartments. I had not seen Mrs. Ainslee for two or three days, and my conscience rather troubled me about her, so that when, on this day—a day that will never fade

from my mind as long as I live, nor from that of
Bera or Swiftwater—I quickly fell into Bera's plans
and determined to get some things together for
Mrs. Ainslee, including a bunch of roses from a
vase on my dresser, and go to the hospital after
dinner.

Providence Hospital was scarcely more than five
blocks from our apartments. I had not seen anything of Swiftwater or Hathaway all day. Tired
even beyond the ordinary—it had been a long, hard
fight to get my affairs in shape for the northern
trip—I left the apartments a little before seven
o'clock that fateful evening and walked up Second
Avenue to Madison and thence up to Fifth Avenue
to Providence Hospital.

"Mrs. Ainslee is feeling some better, Mrs. Beebe.
but the doctor is in there now and you will have to
wait for a few minutes," the head nurse told me at
the landing on the second floor. The steamer "Humboldt" was sailing for Alaska that night, and I had
managed to get off a few things consigned to myself at Dawson and had seen them safely placed
aboard ship.

As I sat waiting for the signal to come into Mrs
Ainslee's room—it must have been a half hour or
more before the nurse came to me and said I should
enter—a curious feeling came over me regarding
Bera. I had never known of her speaking about

Mrs. Ainslee and somehow or other I could not get out of my mind the thought that possibly Swiftwater and his friend Hathaway might leave for Skagway on the "Humboldt."

Philosophers may talk of a woman's sixth sense as some people talk of the cunning of a cat. Whatever it was, as the nurse beckoned me to come into Mrs. Ainslee's room, I quickly arose, went in and said to the sick woman:

"Mrs. Ainslee, I am awfully glad to see that you are better and I wanted to visit with you for an hour, but I have overstayed my time already and I must hurry back to my rooms."

Then I quickly turned and in another minute I was hurrying down the Madison Street hill to the Hinckley Block. In every step I took nearer my home there came a keener and more tense pulling at my heart strings—a feeling that something had happened in my own home. It was no wonder that the elevator boy in the Hinckley Block was dumbfounded to see me rush across Second Avenue and half way up the stairs to the second floor before he could call to me, saying he would take me up in the car if I was not in too big a hurry.

The next moment I was in my rooms, and for the life of me I cannot begin to describe their looks. My clothes and personal belongings were scattered all over the room, my big trunk had been emptied of its contents and was missing. The bureau drawers were empty and the place really looked like a Kansas rancher's house after a cyclone.

On the dresser was a little note—in Bera's handwriting, held down by a bronze paperweight surmounted by a tiny, but beautiful miniature of a woman's form. It was Bera's last birthday gift to me.

"We have gone to Alaska with Swiftwater and Mr. Hathaway. Do not worry, mama, as when we get there we will look out for your hotel."

"BERA."

That was Bera's note. I looked at my watch: It was 7:25 and I knew the "Humboldt" sailed at 8 o'clock. I rushed down four flights of stairs, never thinking of the elevator, gained the street and hailed a passing hackman.

"You can have this if you get to the 'Humboldt' at Schwabacher's dock before she sails!" I cried as the cabby drew his team to the curb, and then I handed him a ten dollar gold piece.

Whipping his horses to a gallop, the hackman drove at a furious pace down First Avenue to Spring Street and thence to the dock. He all but knocked over a policeman as the horses under his whip surged through the crowd which stood around the dock waiting for the departure of the "Humboldt."

"My two daughters are on that boat and Swift-water Bill Gates has stolen them from me!" I shouted as I grabbed hold of the arm of a big police-man near the entrance to the dock. "I want you to get those girls off that boat before she sails, no mat-ter what happens!"

In another minute the policeman was fighting his way with all the force of his 250 pounds through the mob of five thousand people that hung around the gang plank of the "Humboldt." The ship's lights were burning brightly and everybody was laughing and talking, and a few women crying as they said goodby to husbands, sweethearts or friends aboard the ship.

It was just exactly ten minutes before sailing time when we finally made our way to the main deck through the crowd. I fairly shouted to the captain on the bridge:

"My two daughters are on this ship hidden away, and I want them taken off this boat before you leave!"

Capt. Bateman looked at me a moment as if he wanted to throw me overboard.

"Who are your daughters and what are they doing on my ship?"

"My daughters are Blanche and Bera Beebe and Swiftwater Bill has stolen them and is taking them to Alaska. I am Mrs. Beebe, their mother."

For the moment that ended the discussion with Capt. Bateman. Instantly turning to a quartermaster, he said:

"Help this woman find her daughters!"

A half an hour and then an hour passed as we worked our way from one stateroom to another on the saloon deck and the upper deck without avail Capt. Bateman was furious at the delay.

"Mrs. Beebe, I do not believe your daughters are here," he said. "Swiftwater has engaged one room, but we have not seen him yet."

Just then the quartermaster turned to unlock the door of a stateroom on the starboard side near the stern of the ship. The lock failed to work.

"There is somebody in there," he said, "and the dock is locked from the inside."

"Break it in!" ordered Capt. Bateman.

The next instant the door flew off its hinges as the big quartermaster shoved a burly shoulder against it. The room was dark. I rushed in, to find Bera lying on the couch, sobbing as if her heart would break.

As quickly as possible, I got the girls out and turned them over to the custody of Capt. Bateman.

"These are my daughters, and I will not allow them to be taken from me."

"Take 'em ashore!" ordered Capt. Bateman to the quartermaster.

"COME TO THE STATION WITH US," SAID THE OF-
FICER, DRAGGING FORTH THE SHAPELESS MASS,
AND HELPING SWIFTWATER ADJUST HIS SILK TILE.

"But I want you to find that scoundrel Swift-water!" said I, turning on the policeman, who stood just behind me.

"You'll not keep us here any longer," angrily said the ship's master.

"O, yes, we will!" said the officer, showing more grit than I expected.

Then began the search all over again. The hurricane deck was the last resort, the ship having been searched from her hold clear through the steerage and saloon cabins to the main deck.

On the main deck there were a half dozen life-boats securely lashed in their proper places. It was dark by this time, but, curiously enough, there was a little fluttering electric arc light near the end of the warehouse on the dock, close to the after end of the boat.

That lamp must have been burning that night through some of the mysterious and indefinable laws of Providence or some other thing, because by its glare I could see a huddled, shapeless, black form underneath the last lifeboat on the upper deck.

"That's him!" I said, pointing at the shapeless mass in the shadow of the lifeboat.

The policeman walked over to the boat, stretched forth a big muscular arm, grasped the formless object and drew forth—Swiftwater Bill.

"Come to the station with us," said the officer, as he helped Bill adjust his silk tile.

CHAPTER VI.

FULL thirty days after Swiftwater and Hathaway had left Seattle, following the affair on the decks of the steamer "Humboldt," found the miner and his friend in Skagway. It was in the height of the spring rush to the gold fields, and there are undoubtedly few, if any, living today who will ever witness on this continent such scenes as were enacted on the terrible Skagway trail over the Coast Range of the Alaska mountains, which separated 50,000 eager, struggling, quarreling, frenzied men and women drawn thither by the mad rush for gold from the upper reaches of the Yukon River and the lakes which helped to form that mighty stream.

No pen can adequately portray the bitter clash, and struggling, and turmoil—man against man, man against woman, woman against man, fist against fist, gun against gun, as this mob of gold-crazed human beings surged into the vortex of the Yukon's valley and found their way to the new Golconda of the north.

Skagway was a whirling, tumbling, seething whirlpool of humanity. Imagine the spectacle of a mob of 40,000 half-crazed human beings assembled at the foot of the almost impassable White Pass, with the thermometer 90 degrees in the shade at the foot of the range, and ten feet of snow on the Summit, three miles away. Then picture to this, if you can, the innumerable crimes against humanity that broke out in this mob of half-crazy, fighting, excited, bewildered multitude of men and women.

There was no rest in the town—no sleep—no time for meals—no time for repose—nothing but a mad scramble and the devil take the hindmost.

There was one cheap, newly constructed frame hotel in Skagway and rooms were from $5 to $20 a day. The only wharf of the town was packed fifty feet high with merchandise of every description —65 per cent. canned provisions, flour and dried fruits and the rest of it hardware, mining tools and clothing for the prospectors. Teams of yelping, snarling, fighting malamutes added their cries to the eternally welling mass of sound.

And Swiftwater was there. Almost the first face I saw as I entered the hotel was that of Gates.

"Mrs. Beebe," he said, "let us forget bygones. In another day or two I would have been over the Summit with my outfit. It is lucky that I am here, because possibly I can help you in some way."

I could do nothing more than listen to what Swiftwater said. There was no other hotel, or in-

deed any place in the town where I could get shelter
for myself and my two girls. Knowing the black
purpose in Swiftwater's heart, I watched my girls
Bera and Blanche day and night. My own gooos
were piled up unsheltered and unprotected on the
beach.

Swiftwater, with all his cunning, could not de-
ceive me of his real intent, yet my own perplexities
and troubles made it easy for him to keep me in
constant fear of him.

"Mrs. Beebe," he would say, "you can trust me
absolutely."

With that, Swiftwater's face would take on a
smile as innocent as that of a babe. There was
always the warm, soft clasp of the womanish hand
—the low pitched voice of Swiftwater to keep it
company.

And now, as I remember how innocent Bera was,
how girlish she looked, how confiding she was in
me, yet never for a moment forgetting, perhaps, the
lure of the gold studded gravel banks of Eldorado
which Swiftwater held constantly before her, it
seems to my mind that no woman can be wronged as
deeply and as eternally as that woman whose daughter is stolen from her through guile and soft deceit.

We had been in Skagway but a trifle more than a
week, when, one evening, returning to the hotel, I
found my room empty and Bera missing.

"I have gone with Swiftwater to Dawson, Mamma. He loves me and I love him." This was what Bera had written and left on her dresser.

That was all. There was one chance only to prevent the kidnaping of Bera. That was for me to get to the lakes on the other side of the mountains, at the head of navigation on the Yukon and seek the aid of the Canadian mounted police.

At White Horse, there was trace of Swiftwater and Bera, but they had twenty-four hours the start of me and. when I finally found that they had gone through to Dawson, I simply quit.

Down the Upper Yukon there was a constant stream of barges, small boats and rafts. Miles Canyon, with its madly rushing, white-capped waters, extending over five miles of rock-ribbed river bed and sand bar, was scattered o'er with timbers, boards, boxes and casks containing the outfits and all the worldly possessions of scores of unfortunates.

"On, on, and ever and eternally on, down the Yukon to Dawson!" That was the cry in those days and it bore, as unresistingly and as mercilessly as the tide of the ocean carries the flotsam and jetsam of seacoast harbors, the brave and the strong, the weak and crippled, the wise and the foolish, in one inchoate mass of humanity to that magic spot where more gold lay underground waiting for the pick of

the poverty-struck miner than the world had ever
known of—"The Klondike."

All things finally come to an end. I was in Dawson. At the little temporary dock on the Yukon's
bank, stood Bera and Swiftwater. The miner did
not wait till I landed from the little boat. He went
up the gang plank and grasped me in his arms.

"Mrs. Beebe," he said, "we're married. Come
with us to our cabin. We are waiting for you, and
dinner is on the table."

Swiftwater during all that summer and winter in
Dawson was the very soul of chivalry and attention
both to Bera and myself. There was nothing too
good for us in the little market places at Dawson
and a box of candy at $5 a box just to please Bera
or to satisfy my own taste for sweetmeats was no
more to Swiftwater than the average man spending
a two-bit piece on the outside.

As the spring broke up the river and then summer took the place of spring in Dawson, the traders
from the outside brought in supplies of fresh eggs,
fresh oranges, lettuce, new onions—all the delica-
cies greatly to be prized and more esteemed after a
long winter than the rarest fruits and dainties of
the States.

When summer came, Dawson got its first shipment
of new watermelons from the outside, Swiftwater

bought the first melon he could find and paid $40 in dust for it, and brought it home, simply to please Bera and to make his home that much happier.

CHAPTER VII.

HYDRAULIC mining in the Klondike country, by the time that Swiftwater had assembled his big outfit on Quartz Creek was in its very infancy, yet there were plenty of wise men in Dawson who knew that the tens of thousands of acres of hillside slopes and old abandoned creek beds would some day produce more gold when washed into sluice boxes with gigantic rams, than the native miner and prospector had been able to show, even with the figures, $50,000,000, output to his credit.

The Canadian government had given Swiftwater and his partner, Joe Boyle, a princely fortune in the three mile concession on Quartz Creek. So great was the reputation of Swiftwater Bill—so intimately was his name linked with the idea of immense quantities of gold—and so high was his standing as a practical miner, that Swiftwater was able to borrow money right and left to carry on his work on Quartz Creek. Thus it was that before anybody could realize it, including myself, Swiftwater's financial standing actually was $100,000 worse off than nothing. This was about the amount of money that he used and in that tidy sum was all the savings of my winter in Dawson and my dividends from my hotel, which aggregated at least $35,000.

"When Joe comes in this spring from London," said Swiftwater to me, "we'll have all the money we want and more, too, Mrs. Beebe. He has cabled twice to Seattle that our money is all raised and we will have a million-dollar clean-up on Quartz Creek this fall."

As the spring came on and reports from the mines on Quartz Creek became brighter, Swiftwater became more enthusiastic and confident. The fact that his creditors were beginning to worry, and that there is a nasty law in Canada which affects debtors who seek to leave the country in a restraining way, did not seriously worry Swiftwater. He seemed to think more of the coming of his child than anything else, next to the work on Quartz Creek.

"That baby is going to be born on Quartz Creek, Mrs. B—" Swiftwater said. "It is my determination that my first child shall be born where I will make a greater fortune than anybody hereabouts."

I told Swiftwater that he was talking arrant nonsense.

"It would be the death of Bera in her condition," said I, "for her to take the trip up there in this cold, nasty weather, with the roads more like swamps than anything else and the hills still covered with

snow. More than that, there are doctors here in
Dawson and on Quartz Creek we would be thirty
miles from the nearest human settlement.''

But nothing would deter Swiftwater. He set
about rigging up a big sled which could be pulled
by two horses. It was made of heavy oaken
timber, and the long low bed was filled with
furs, blankets, bedding, etc. Swiftwater went
to Dr. Marshall, our physician, when all ar-
rangements had been practically completed for the
journey to Quartz. He had effectually stopped my
protests before he said to Dr. Marshall:

''I will give you $2,000 or more, if necessary, to
take six weeks off and go with me up to Quartz
Creek where my child will be born. Just name your
figure if that is not enough.''

Bera was seventeen years old, immature and deli-
cate, yet brave and strong, and willing to imperil
her own life to gratify Swiftwater's whim. So it
finally came about that I was delegated to do the
final shopping in advance of our journey.

I went to Gandolfo's and bought with my own
money a case of oranges and a crate of apples. Each
orange cost $3 in dust and the apples about the same.
Next I ordered a barrel of bottled beer, for Swiftwater wanted to treat his men with a feast when the
baby was born and the bottled beer was what he

BERA BEEBE GATES
From a photograph taken at Washington, D. C., where she was deserted by Swiftwater Bill.

thought to be the proper thing. The barrel of beer cost me close to $500 in gold.

All this stuff was loaded on the sled. They started over the twenty-eight miles of crooked, winding, marshy trail to Quartz Creek. The journey was something terrible. The days were short and the wind from the hills and gulches was wet with the thawing of the snow and so cold that it seemed to make icicles of the drippings from the trees. Bera, wrapped a foot thick in furs, seemed to stand the trip all right, and in due time the baby was born and christened.

There was great rejoicing in the camp and Swift-water weighed out $3,000 in dust to Dr. Marshall and sent him back to Dawson. A month afterwards one of our men brought from Dawson the word that the mail had arrived over the ice, but Swiftwater looked in vain for a letter from Joe Boyle. He had confidently expected a draft for $50,000.

For two days Swiftwater scarcely spoke. The cabin in which we lived was only a quarter of a mile from the nearest dump where the men were working. I used to go out every once in a while and take up a few shovels full of gravel which would wash out between $5 and $10 and if I had had the good common sense which comes only after years of hard knocks in this troublesome world, I could then and there have protected myself against the bitter misfortunes which came to me in a few months afterwards.

I was washing some of the baby's clothes in the kitchen and drying them on a line over the fire, when Swiftwater came in from the diggings, clad in his rubber boots which reached to his hips.

The miner asked for some hot water and a towel and began to shave the three weeks' black growth from his chin.

"What are you going to do now, Swiftwater?" I asked.

"I'm going down to town."

For two days the cabin had been without food except some mush and a few dried potatoes and a can of condensed milk for the baby. Swiftwater had sent a man over the trail to Dawson for food two days before.

"You'll not go without Bera! You are not going to leave us here to starve," said I.

"Bera cannot possibly go," said Bill.

I turned and went to Bera's room and told her to dress immediately. Then I washed the baby, put an entire new change of clothes on him, wrapped up his freshly ironed garments in a package, got a bottle of soothing syrup and a can of condensed milk.

It was always my belief and is now, that Swiftwater's mind contained a plan to abandon Bera, the baby and me, and to run away from the Yukon to escape his troubles.

We got a small boat and filled one end of it with fir boughs, covered them over with rugs, and put Bera and the baby there. Then Swiftwater and I got in the boat and pushed off down stream.

Swiftwater confessed to me for the first time that he was in serious trouble.

"There have been three strange men from Dawson out here on our claims," said Swiftwater, "and I know who sent them out. They are watching me."

As I look back upon that awful trip down Indian River, with poor, wan, white-faced Bera hugging the little three weeks' old baby to her bosom, so sick that she could hardly talk, I wonder if there is any hardship, and peril, and privation, and suffering, a woman cannot endure.

The boat was heavy—terribly heavy. In the small stretches of still water it was desperately hard, bone-racking toil to keep moving.

In the rushes of the river, where rapids tore at mill-race speed over boulders and pebbly stretches, we were constantly in danger of being upset. An hour of this sort of work made me almost ready for any sort of fate.

Finally we struck a big rock and the current carried us on a stretch of sandy beach. Swiftwater and I got out and waded up to our armpits in the

cold stream to get the boat started again. Then
we climbed aboard and once more shot down the
rocky canyon to another stretch of still water beyond. By nightfall we had reached an old cabin
half way to Dawson, in which the fall before Swiftwater had cached provisions. The baby's food was
all gone, and Bera, in a fit of anger, had thrown
what little bread and butter sandwiches we had
put up for ourselves, overboard. I had not eaten
all day, nor had Swiftwater.

It was growing dusk when we painfully pulled
the boat on the bank at Swiftwater's cache. Gates
went inside to get some grub and prepared to build
a fire. He came out a moment later, his face ashy
pale, his eyes downcast.

"They have stolen all I had put in here," he said.

It seemed to me that night as if the very limit of
human misery on this earth was my bitter portion
as we waited all through the weary hours in the
cabin huddled before a little fire, waiting (it is light
all the time in summer) to resume our journey to
Dawson.

The next day we reached Dawson shortly after
noon, famished, cold, and completely exhausted. I
actually believe the baby would have died but for
the bottle of soothing syrup and water which I had
brought along.

Swiftwater took us to the Fairview Hotel and sent
for the doctor for Bera and the baby.

CHAPTER VIII.

O THE people of Dawson, in those days, starving through weary winter months for want of frequent mail communication with the civilized world, and hungering for the ebb and flow of human tide that is a natural and daily part of the lives of those in more fortunate places, the arrival of the first steamer from "the outside" in the spring is an event even greater than a Fourth of July celebration to a country town in Kansas.

For days before our arrival down Indian River from Quartz Creek, the men and women of Dawson had eagerly discussed the probability of the coming of the Yukoner, the regular river liner from White Horse due any moment, with fresh provisions from Seattle and the first papers and letters from "the outside."

For two days after Swiftwater had taken Bera to the Fairview Hotel, the doctor had cared for her so as to enable her to recover from the hardships of the trip down Indian River. I took the baby to my own rooms and carefully nursed him through all one day. This brought him quickly round, and he soon looked as bright and cheerful as a new twenty dollar gold piece.

It was on the third morning after we arrived in Dawson that the steamer Yukoner's whistle sounded up the river, and the whole populace rushed to the wharves and river banks. Miners came from all points up the creeks to welcome friends or to get their mail that the Yukoner had brought. The little shopkeepers in Dawson, particularly the fruit venders, were extremely active, bustling amongst the crowd on the dock and fighting their way to get the first shipments of early vegetables, fruits, fresh eggs, fresh butter and other perishable commodities for which Dawson hungered.

But Swiftwater, keen eyed, nervous, straining, yet trying to be composed, saw none of this, nor felt the least interest in the tide of newcomers who stepped from the Yukoner's decks and made their way up town surrounded by friends.

Swiftwater was looking for one face in the crowd —that of his partner, Joe Boyle, who had promised to bring him $100,000 from London, where the big concession on Quartz Creek had been bonded for $250,000.

Swiftwater stood at the gang plank and eagerly scanned every face until the last man had come ashore and only the deck hands remained on board.

"There is certainly a letter in the mail, anyhow," said Swiftwater.

For the first time in all of this miserable experi-

ence I realized that a heavy burden was on Swiftwater's shoulders—a load that was crushing the
heart and brain of him—and that would, unless re-
lieved, destroy all of the man's native capacity to
handle his tangled affairs, even under the most un-
favorable circumstances.

I decided to watch Swiftwater very closely. I
noticed that he was not to be seen around town in
his usual haunts. I did not dare ask him if he
feared arrest, for that would show that I knew
that his crisis had come.

Two hours after the Yukoner's mail was in the
postoffice, Swiftwater came to my room.

"There is no letter from Joe," was all he said.

I made no reply except to say:

"Have you told Bera?"

"No, and I'm not going to—now," said Swiftwater and then left the room.

Swiftwater had between $35,000 and $40,000 of
my money in his Quartz Creek concession. I had
felt absolutely secure for the reason that if the property was well handled my interest should be worth
from $100,000 to $250.000. My faith in the property
has been justified by subsequent events, as all well
informed Dawson mining men will testify.

But the want of money was bitter and keen at
that moment. Yet I scarcely know what to advise
Swiftwater to do.

Gates and Bera came to my rooms after dinner that night.

"Will this help you pay a few pressing little bills?" asked Swiftwater, as he threw two fifty dollar paper notes in my lap.

"My God, Swiftwater, can't you spare any more than $100?" I gasped.

"Oh, that's just for now—I'll give you plenty more tomorrow," said he.

As they arose to go, Bera kissed me on the mouth and cheek with her arms around my neck.

"You love the baby, don't you mama?" said Bera, and I saw then, without seeing, and came afterwards to know that there were tears in Bera's eyes and a smile dewy with affection on her lips.

Swiftwater put his arm around me and kissed me on the forehead

"We'll be over early for you for breakfast to-morrow," said Swiftwater as they went down the stairs.

Holding the baby in my arms at the window, I watched Swiftwater and Bera go down the street, Bera turning now and again to wave her hand and throw a kiss to me, Swiftwater lifting his hat.

Now, what I am about to relate may seem almost incredible to any normal human mind and heart; and especially so to those thousands of Alaskans who knew Swiftwater in the early days to be jolly, though impractical, yet always generous, whole-souled, brave and honest.

An hour after Swiftwater and Bera had gone, there was a knock at my door. I opened it and there stood Phil Wilson—an old associate and friend of Swiftwater's.

"Is Bill Gates here?" asked Wilson.

"Why, no," said I. "They went over an hour ago."

"Thank you," said he, and lumbered heavily down the stairs.

The next morning I waited until 11 o'clock for Swiftwater and Bera to come for me to go to breakfast. I had slept little or none the night before and my nerves were worn down to the fine edge that comes just before a total collapse.

When it seemed as if I could not wait longer, there came a knock at the door.

When I opened the door there stood George Taylor, a friend of Swiftwater's of some years' standing.

"Mrs. Beebe, I came to tell you that Swiftwater and Bera left early this morning to go to Quartz Creek on horseback. I promised Swiftwater I would help you move to his cabin and get everything ready for their return on Saturday."

"In Heaven's name, what is Swiftwater trying to do—kill Bera?" I exclaimed. "That ride to

Quartz Creek in her condition, through the mud and mire of that trail, will kill her."

Taylor merely looked at me and did not answer.

"Are you telling me the truth?" I demanded.

"I am," he said.

Taylor walked away and I closed the door and went back to the baby.

"Baby," said I, "I guess we're left all alone for a while and you haven't any mama but me."

Although I afterward learned of the fact, it did me no good at that trying moment that Swiftwater had told Bera, before she would consent to leave me, that he had sent me $800 in currency by Wilson. Of course, Swiftwater did nothing of the kind, yet his story was such as to lead Bera to believe that I was well protected and comfortable.

Then I set to work to move my little belongings into Swiftwater's cabin, there to wait for four days hoping that every minute would bring some word from Bera and Gates. There was little to eat in the cabin and the $100 that Swiftwater had given me had nearly all gone for baby's necessities. The little fellow had kept up well and strong in spite of everything, and when I undressed him at night and bathed him and got him ready for his bed, he seemed so brave and strong and sweet that I could not, for the life of me, give way to the feeling of desolation and loss that my circumstances warranted.

On the third day after Bera and Swiftwater had gone and I was getting a little supper for the baby and myself in the cabin, there came a clatter of heavy boots on the gravel walk in front of the house and a boisterous knock on the door.

Jumping up from the kitchen table, I nearly ran to the door, believing that Bera and Swiftwater were there. Instead there stood a messenger from the McDonald Hotel in Dawson with a letter for me. It simply said:

"We have gone down the river in a small boat to Nome with Mr. Wilson. I will send you money immediately on arrival there, so that you can join us. SWIFTWATER."

That was all.

I read the letter through again and then the horror of it came over me—I all alone in Dawson with Swiftwater's four weeks' old baby, broke and he owing me nearly $40,000.

Then everything seemed to leave me and I fell to the floor unconscious. Hours afterward—they said it was 9 o'clock at night, and the messenger had been there at 4 in the afternoon—I came to. The baby was crying and hungry. It seemed to me I had been in a long sickness and I could not for a while quite realize where I was or what ill shape of a hostile fate had befallen me. And, when I think of it now, it seems to me any other woman in my place would have gone crazy.

For two months I stayed in that cabin, trying my best to find a way out of Dawson and unable to move a rod because of the fact that I had no money. Swiftwater, as I learned afterwards, took a lay on a claim on Dexter Creek and cleaned up in a short time $4,000.

When I heard this, I wrote to him for money for the baby, but none came.

A month passed and then another and no word from Swiftwater. I felt as long as I had a roof over my head, I could make a living for myself and the baby by working at anything—manicuring, hair-dressing or sewing. Then, one evening, just after I had finished dinner, came a rap at the door.

It was Phil Wilson.

"Swiftwater has given me a deed to this house and power of attorney over his other matters," said he. "I shall move my things over here and occupy one of these three rooms."

I knew better than to make any objection then, but the next day I told Wilson:

"You will have to take your things down town— you cannot stay here."

"I guess I'll stay all right, Mrs. Beebe," said he.

"And it will be all winter, too. And, I think it would be better for you, Mrs. Beebe, if you stayed here with me."

I knew just what that meant. I said:

"Mr. Wilson, I understand you, but you will go and take your things now."

Wilson left in another minute and I did not see him for two days. On the second afternoon I locked the door with a padlock and went down town to do some shopping for the baby, who I had left with a neighbor. I also wanted to send a fourth letter to Swiftwater, begging him to send me some money to keep me and his baby from starving.

When I got back at dusk that evening, the door to the cabin was broken open, and the chain and padlock lay on the ground shattered into fragments.

I went inside. All my clothes, the baby's and even the little personal belongings of the child were piled together in a disordered heap in the center room.

CHAPTER IX.

IT WAS pitch dark when I left the cabin and made my way directly, as best I could, to the town with its dimly lighted streets. It seemed to me that I had never had a friend in all this world. Friend? Yes, FRIEND. That is to say—a human being who could be depended upon in any emergency and who was right—right all the time in fair as well as in foul weather.

There was only one thought in my mind—that was to find some man or woman in all that country to whom I could go for shelter and for aid. I knew naught of Swiftwater and Bera, except that they had left me. Swiftwater's child, I felt as if he was my own—that little babe smiling up into my face as I had held him in my arms but a few minutes before, seemed to me as if he was my own.

I knew instinctively that there was none in all that multitude of carefree or careworn miners who thronged the three cafes and the dance halls of Dawson who could do much, if anything, to help me.

Past the dance halls and saloons and gambling halls of Dawson I went my way, down beyond the town and finally found the dark trail that led to the barracks of the mounted police. I told the captain exactly what had happened. I said:

"Captain, I am left all alone here by Swiftwater Bill and I have to find some place to shelter his little two months' old child and to feed and clothe him. He told me to live in his cabin. But I have no home there now as long as that man Wilson lives there."

No woman who has never known the hard and seamy side of life in Dawson can possibly understand how good are the mounted police to every human being, man, woman or child, who is in trouble without fault of their own. The captain said:

"Mrs. Beebe, I have long known of you, and I do not doubt that a wrong has been done you. You and your little grandson shall not suffer for want of shelter or food tonight."

With that the captain detailed two officers with instructions to accompany me to Swiftwater's cabin and to see that I was comfortably and safely housed there, no matter what the circumstances. We went back that long, dark way, a mile over the trail to the cabin. When we arrived there, the two officers went inside.

"Place this woman's clothes and belongings where they were before you came in here, and do it at once," commanded one of the mounted police.

Wilson looked at me in amazement, and then his face was flushed with an angry glow as he saw that the two officers meant business.

Without a word, he picked up all the baby's clothes and my own and put them back where they had been before. Then he took his pack of clothes and belongings and left without a word.

It would merely encumber my story to tell how I was summoned into court by Phil Wilson, and how. the judge, after. hearing my story of Swiftwater's brutality—of his leaving me in Dawson penniless with his baby—said that he could hardly conceive how a man could be so inhuman as Swiftwater was, to leave the unprotected mother of his wife and his baby alone in such a place as Dawson and in such hands as those of the man who stood before him. He said that such brutality, in his judgment, was without parallel in Dawson's annals and that, while he felt the deepest sympathy for me, left as I had been helpless and with Swiftwater's baby, yet the law gave Phil Wilson the right to the cabin.

This ended the case. I turned to go from the courtroom when the Presbyterian minister, Dr. McKenzie, came to me and said:

"Mrs. Beebe, I do not know anything about the circumstances that have brought you to this condition, but if you will let me have the child I will see that he has a good home and is well cared for."

But this was not necessary, as it turned out afterwards, because Dr. McKenzie took the matter up with the council, where it was threshed out in all its details. The council voted $125 a month for sustenance for the nurse and the baby. The mounted police took me to the barracks and there provided a cabin and food, with regular supplies of provisions from the canteen.   ,

I do not doubt but that the monthly expense during the winter that I lived there with the baby is still a matter of record in Dawson in the archives of the government, and I am equally certain that, although Swiftwater Bill has made hundreds of thousands of dollars since that day and is now reputed to be worth close to $1,000,000, he has never liquidated the debt he owes to the Canadian government for the care and sustenance and shelter they gave his own boy. All of the facts stated in this chapter can easily be verified by recourse to the records of the court and mounted police in Dawson.

Although I knew that Swiftwater was making money in Nome, I placed no more dependence in him from that moment and managed to sustain myself by manicuring and hairdressing in Dawson.

The winter wore away, and there was the usual annual celebration of the coming of spring with

its steamers from White Horse laden with the first
papers and the mail from the outside. In May of
that year I received a telegram from Swiftwater
Bill telling me to leave Dawson on the first boat
and come down the river to Nome, as he and Bera
would be there on the first boat from Seattle. The
day after I received the telegram the mail came
and brought a letter written by Swiftwater from
Chicago, saying that he had the money to pay me
all he owed me and more too, and for me not to
fail to meet him and Bera in Nome.

Isn't it curious how a woman will forget all the
injustice she suffers at the hands of a man, when
it seems to her that he is trying to do and is doing
the right thing?

Does it seem odd to you, my woman reader, that
the thought of meeting Bera again and of giving
to her and to Swiftwater the custody of the dear
little child I had loved and nursed all winter long,
should have appealed to me?

And now, as there must be an end to the hardest
luck story—just as there is a finish at some time
to all forms of human grief and sorrow—so there
came an end to that winter in the little cabin near
the mounted police barracks at Dawson, where baby
and I and the nurse, Lena Hubbell, had spent so
many weeks waiting for a change in our luck.

Again there was a mob of every kind of people in Dawson.

On the first steamer leaving Dawson I went with the child, after giving up a good business that netted me between $200 and $300 a month. I took the nurse girl with me—who had been in unfortunate circumstances in Dawson—and I speak of her now, as she figures prominently in another chapter in this book.

It matters little now that Swiftwater could have provided handsomely for me and the child—that he took the money that he made from his lay on Dexter Creek and spent it gambling at Nome; and that Bera, knowing my circumstances, took from a sluice box on his claim enough gold to exchange for $500 in bills at Nome, to send to me.

And when I think of this my blood boils, for Bera, after she had the $500 in bills wrapped in a piece of paper and sealed up in an envelope addressed to me, met Swiftwater on the street in Nome and he took the money away from her, saying:

"Bera, I'll mail that letter to your mother."

Of course, I never got the money because Swiftwater gambled it away, and I laying awake nights crying and unable to sleep because of my worry, and working hard throughout the long winter days to support Swiftwater's child.

So it came about that we boarded the big river steamer Susie for Nome. Her decks were jammed with people eager to get outside or anxious to try their fortunes in the new Seward Peninsula gold fields or the beach diggings at Nome. The Yukon was clear of ice, wide, deep and beautiful to look upon in summer, though in winter, when the ice is packed up one hundred feet high, it carries the death dealing blizzards that bring an untimely fate to many a hardy traveler.

In Nome I found no further news of Swiftwater nor Bera and waited there for three weeks. Then, after days of watching at the postoffice, I got a letter from Swiftwater, saying that it would not be possible for him to come to Nome, and there was not even so much as a dollar bill in the letter.

Disheartened and miserable, I turned to go back to my hotel. As I turned from the postoffice a news-boy rushed up from the wharf, crying out:

"SEATTLE TIMES—ALL ABOUT SWIFT-WATER BILL RUNNING AWAY WITH AN-OTHER WOMAN."

CHAPTER X.

S I write this chapter, which is to interest not only the friends and acquaintances of Swiftwater Bill, but which also may throw a new light on his character, and may even arouse a general interest in the odd freaks of human nature which one finds in the northern country, I am moved to wonder whether or not there is a human pen capable of portraying all of the many-sided phases of Swiftwater's nature. The story in the Seattle paper merely gave an outline of Swiftwater's escapade, when he ran away with Kitty Brandon, took her from Portland to Seattle and back to Chehalis and there married her on June 20th, 1901.

If Swiftwater Bill's title as the Don Juan of the Klondike had ever been questioned before this affair, it seems to me that his elopement with Kitty Brandon from Portland early in June of that year would have forever settled the matter in his favor. The Seattle paper merely told that Swiftwater and Kitty had been married, against the will and wish of her mother at Chehalis, and that the girl's mother learning of the affair had followed the lovers to Seattle.

Kitty was a fragile, neatly formed girl of fifteen years, when she went to St. Helen's Hall in Portland

as a student. Swiftwater left Bera in the spring
of that year at Washington, D. C., and hurried
across the continent, intending, as he told me in all
his letters, on making another fortune in Alaska.
He had valuable interests in the gold mining district
near Teller, Alaska, and in his fond imagination
there was every reason to believe that the Kougarok
country was as rich, if not richer, than Eldorado
and Bonanza in the Klondike.

"Bring my baby down to Nome and meet me
at Teller," Swiftwater wrote me. "I am so glad
you have taken such good care of my darling son
all winter in Dawson. I shall pay you all that
you have loaned me and I will see that you make
more money in Teller City than you ever made in
Dawson. I could hug and kiss you for taking such
good care of our baby boy."

Such was the language of Swiftwater's letters to
me, written in Washington in the spring of that
year. Swiftwater reasoned that all of Alaska is
underlaid with gold; that the fabulous riches of
Eldorado and Bonanza would be duplicated again
and again on Seward peninsula. To his mind, the
making of a fortune of a million of dollars in a
summer in the new diggings near Teller was one
of the simplest things in the world, and it is not to
be wondered at that there were hundreds among
his friends who believed then and do now that his

mining judgment and fairy-like luck were such as to enable him to go forth into the north at any time and bring out hundreds of thousands of dollars in the precious yellow stuff.

Be that as it may, when Swiftwater reached the coast, he happened by ill chance to stop at Portland. In St. Helen's Hall there was Kitty Brandon, known as his niece, a girl of more than ordinary mental and physical charms. Once again the amorous nature of Swiftwater Bill asserted itself. It is related that he called at St. Helen's Hall and interviewed Kitty Brandon, and then after that was a frequent visitor, taking Kitty at odd times driving through the beautiful city of Portland or entertaining her at lunch or dinner, as the case might be, in Portland's swell cafes.

That Swiftwater had no plans for his immediate future can well be believed when it is known that after a few days of courtship of Kitty Brandon, he eloped with the little girl and came to Seattle. On the way to Seattle Kitty and Swiftwater were married at Chehalis.

It is not surprising that Swiftwater found his last love affair anything but a summer holiday, when it is remembered that his legal wife, Bera, was in Washington, D. C., awaiting his return. Considerations of propriety and, even of the law, seemed

to have left Swiftwater's mind entirely, until Kitty's
mother learned of his elopement and followed the
loving pair to Seattle.

What followed afterwards was told in the Seattle,
Tacoma and Portland newspapers of that time.
Learning that Swiftwater and Kitty were registered
as man and wife at a Seattle hotel, Kitty's mother
followed them and sought to apprehend them. Then
it was that Swiftwater evinced that capacity for re-
source and tact which, as all his friends know, is
one of his most distinguished characteristics.

With the irate mother of his newest love lying
in wait at night in the lobby of one of Seattle's
best known hotels, it was Swiftwater's task to show
that skill in maneuver and celerity in action which
tens of thousands of Northerners attributed to him
as the origin of his odd nick-name. There was no
time to repent for his infatuation for the pretty
Kitty Brandon, or to remember the fate of his deserted wife and child in Washington.

And Swiftwater was equal to the emergency.
Bidding Kitty's mother wait in the hotel parlor,
Swiftwater rushed to his room, telephoned for a
hack to come to the rear of the hostelry, and in less
than ten minutes Bill and his sweetheart were being
driven at breakneck speed through the streets of
Seattle, southward over the bridge across the tide
flats, headed for Tacoma. It was told by Swiftwater

ESCAPE AT NIGHT OF SWIFTWATER AND KITTY
BRANDON FROM THE GIRL'S IRATE MOTHER.

afterwards that in nearly every mile of that trip
fear that Kitty's mother was pursuing him and his
inamorita followed him and for the greater part of
the way he kept watching down the dark road in the
rear of his hack, expecting that at every turn of
the road the wrathful parent would be in sight in
readiness to pounce upon him.

From Tacoma, where Swiftwater and Kitty found
only temporary shelter, the runaway pair escaped to
Portland, to return to Seattle and spend their honey-
moon in a little cottage in an obscure district near
Interbay.

CHAPTER XI.

A S I look back on that day in Nome and recall the sensation created in the little mining camp when the paper containing the
story of Swiftwater's perfidy was circu-
lated abroad among the people, I am tempted
to wonder if the duplicate or parallel of
Swiftwater's enormities at this time can be found
in all the annals of this great Northwestern country. The Times' story seemed, even to those like
myself, who knew something of Swiftwater's character, to be almost incredible, and for my part it
was several hours before I realized, in a dumb un-
feeling sort of a way, that Swiftwater had absolutely stolen his own sister's child—Kitty Brandon
—a girl not more than sixteen years old, had eloped
with her, committed bigamy by marrying her in
Chehalis, Wash., and at the same time had deserted
his wife and left her penniless in Washington, D. C.

It was long after nightfall as I sat in my room,
the baby sound asleep in his little crib, the nurse
gone for the night, and I had read The Times'
story about Swiftwater and Kitty over the twentieth
time, that I felt the real force of the shame and
scandal which the miner had placed about himself
and Bera, and which did not even leave me and my

little grandson, Clifford, outside of its dark and forbidding pall.

All that night I lay awake and wondered how in Heaven's name I could get word to Bera—or if she had received a telegram from friends in Seattle and the blow had killed her—or whether she was then on her way West, or whatever fate had befallen her.

I knew little about Swiftwater's business affairs just at that time except that he had gone to Washington in the hope of furthering his mining ventures in the North and had taken Bera with him. Then I remembered that in his letters to me and telegrams urging me to join him at Nome he had spoken about having raised considerable money and was able to pay his debt to me and lift me out of the mire of toil and drudgery in Alaska, in which I had sojourned for so many months.

All that night I neither slept nor rested. It seemed to me at times as if my head would split into a thousand pieces with the thought of Swiftwater's treachery to Bera and myself. Then I realized the utter futility and helplessness of a woman situated as I was in Nome, absolutely unable to get a telegram or quick letter to Bera or to hear from her telling me of her condition. For aught I knew, she might have been deathly sick, cared for only by strangers or left destitute at some place in the East and without any means whatever of righting herself.

It seems to me, now when I think of that all night's vigil in the little hotel in Nome, that Providence must have been watching over me, that I did not lose my reason. At last I found that unless I went to work doing something, I would sure go crazy, and then I started to get work, first borrowing some money, which I sent out by mail the next day to Bera at her last address.

While I worked and slaved in Nome trying to get a few dollars ahead so that I could care for the baby and make my way out to Seattle to help Bera, I finally got word that she had been left destitute in Washington, D. C. Swiftwater had furnished four nice rooms in an apartment house at Washington, and in their effects was more than $1,000 worth of rare curios and ivory from Alaska. Then came another letter that Bera, unable to pay for her care, food and medical attention—the second baby boy was born August 28th—had been put on board a train with a charity ticket, her ivories and curios sold for a trifle and had been started West for Seattle.

I need not dwell on how Bera, more dead than alive from five days traveling in a chair car from Washington to Seattle with her babe at her bosom and unable to sleep at all—with nothing to eat but a few sandwiches which they had given her at Washington—arrived in Seattle and was cared for by friends.

They took the girl, so weak she could hardly stand on her feet, to a restaurant and gave her her first hot meal in almost a week. Then Bera and her baby went to Portland to live with her grandma, while Swiftwater and Kitty Gates were touring the country.

And do you know that Swiftwater's polygamous wife, Kitty Gates, was the girl who Bera one year before had fitted out with a nice outfit of clothes and had sent her to a convent school at Portland to be given a good education?

Yes, this is the truth, and this was Kitty's gratitude to Bera and Swiftwater's crime against the law and his own flesh and blood.

How we managed after I came to Seattle from Nome to live in a little room in a small old fashioned house on Fourth Avenue with barely enough to eat and scarcely enough clothes to cover ourselves need not be told here in detail. I sometimes wonder whether or not I have overladen my little narrative with grief and misery and crime against humanity and against human laws, as well as God's. And then I wonder still more why it was that there were men in Seattle, in San Francisco and in Fairbanks in those days who were always ready to exalt

Swiftwáter and do him honor and take him by the hand, while the world would look askance at Bera Gates, his wife, whom he had so grieviously wronged.

CHAPTER XII.

"SWIFTWATER BILL GATES is back."
One morning in Seattle months after Bera and I had set up a little housekeeping establishment in Seattle, I picked up the Saturday evening edition of The Times and almost dropped over in my chair when I saw headlines in the paper as shown in the foregoing.

What had been Swiftwater Bill's fortune in all those months, I knew not, but the fact as stated in the paper that he had returned from Alaska was sufficient for me.

Bera said: 'Mama, I don't know any reason why you should fuss around about Swiftwater."

"Never mind me," said I, "I'll find him, my dear, just to see what he has to say for himself."

Down to the Hotel Northern, then the Butler, the Rainier-Grand and the Stevens and all the rest I went and searched the registers without avail. As I remember now, it took me the greater part of a day to cover all the ground.

Finally, by a curious chance I located Swiftwater at the Victoria Hotel. I waited until the next morning and then went to the Victoria and asked for Gates.

Swiftwater, the clerk said, was out—had not been seen but once since his arrival.

I am not going to say whether or not it was the humor of the situation or the bitter resentment I bore toward him that led me to tramp up three flights of stairs to the little parlor on the landing close to Swiftwater's room, and to wait there ten hours at a stretch—until 1:10 in the morning. Then I went home, only to return at 8 o'clock the next day.

"Mr. Gates is in his room, but he is asleep," said the clerk

"I am Mrs. Beebe, his mother-in-law, and I want to see him now and I shall go direct to his room. You can go with me if you desire," said I. The little clerk scanned me carefully and then said, "Very well." We went upstairs together.

The clerk rapped on the door twice. There was no answer.

"I guess he's out," said the boy.

"Knock again—good and loud," I commanded.

The boy rapped and just then the door opened a tiny way—about an inch, I guess, but through that little crack I saw the eye and part of the curling black moustache of Swiftwater Bill.

Then I threw myself against the door and walked in.

I wish I could tell you how funny was Swift-

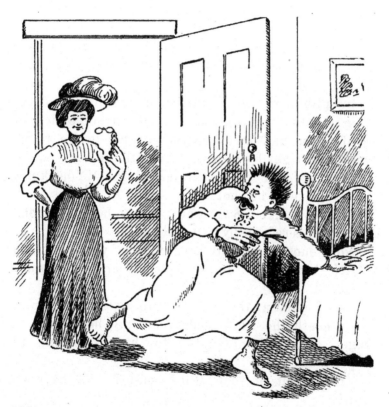

"COME OUT OF THAT, BILL! I HAVEN'T GOT A GUN."

water's apparition, as, clad only in his white night robe, he jumped into bed, pulling the covers over his head.

This was the first time that Swiftwater had seen me since he left me in Dawson alone and unprotected, to find means as best I could to provide shelter and sustenance for his little baby boy, Clifford.

In spite of myself, I laughed, forgetting all of the long months that we had waited for some sign of Swiftwater and an indication of his desire to do what was right by his own two little babies.

"Coward," I said, still laughing. "You know you deserve to be shot."

No answer from Swiftwater, whose body was completely covered up by bed clothes.

Now, most men and most women will admire a MAN, but a cur and a coward are universally despised.

As I looked at that huddled up mass of humanity underneath the white bedspread, my heart rose in rage. The contempt I felt for him is beyond all expression.

"Come out of that, Bill," said I. "I have no gun!"

After a while, Swiftwater poked his head from beneath the bed clothes and showed a blanched face covered with a three weeks' old growth of black

beard. I told him to dress and I would wait outside. In a few minutes Swiftwater emerged and
there stood a man who had commanded hundreds of
thousands of dollars in money and gold in Alaska,
looking just exactly as if he had dropped from the
brake-beam of a Northern Pacific freight train and
had walked his way into Seattle. He was clad in
a dirty sack coat, that shone like a mirror, with
brown striped trousers, an old brown derby hat
and shoes that were out at the sole and side.

"Mrs. Beebe," said Swiftwater in a trembling
voice, "I am all in. If you will not have me arrested, but will give me a chance, I'll soon provide
for the babies and Bera."

Swiftwater pleaded as if for his life. He said
that he could get money in San Francisco from a
man who had offered to back him in a new scheme
in the Tanana country.

There was I with the two little boys and Bera
all on my hands. I told Swiftwater that I would do
nothing for him, but that I would forego having
him put behind steel bars until I' had made up my
mind just what course I should take.

The next night, there was a knock at our door
about 3 o'clock in the morning. Bera slept in the
front room of our little two-room apartment and I
in the other with the babies. I went to the door—
there stood Swiftwater.

"Mrs. Beebe," he said, "I have no place to sleep tonight. If you will let me lie down on the floor, so that I can get a little sleep, I will get up early tomorrow morning and not bother you."

I told Bera to come into my room and I let Swiftwater into the kitchen, where I gave him a comforter on which to lie. The next morning, after Bera had gone, I prepared Swiftwater's breakfast. The man was in rags, almost. I made him take a bath, while I washed his underclothes, and then I went out and bought him a new pair of socks and gave him money with which to buy a new hat.

The next day Swiftwater went to San Francisco on money I furnished him after I had pawned my diamonds with one of the best jewelry houses in Seattle.

Why? Well, because Swiftwater had made me believe that he had another chance in the Tanana and that his friends in San Francisco, having faith in his judgment as a miner—whatever may be said of Swiftwater, he was known throughout the North as an expert miner—had raised a large sum with which to grubstake him.

I will say this for Swiftwater: that he gave me a contract providing that he should pay what he owed me and give me an interest in such mines as he would locate in the Tanana country. And then he went away.

CHAPTER XIII.

OMETIMES, when I recall the stirring events in Swiftwater Bill's career, following the time he used the money I raised by pawning my diamonds and then went to California, I am tempted to wonder whether or not a man of his type of mental makeup ever realized that the hard bumps that he gets along the corduroy road of adversity are one and all of his own making. For, if one will but pause a moment and analyze the events in Swiftwater Bill's melodramatic career, the inevitable result comes to him, namely, that the bumps over which Swiftwater traveled during all of those years, when, one day he was worth a half million dollars in gold, and the next was hiding in all manner of dark and subterranean recesses in order to avoid deputy sheriffs and constables with writs and court processes, were placed there by his own hands and as skilfully and effectively as if he had deliberately planned to cause himself misery.

Swiftwater's transformation from a broken down tramp of the Weary Willie order to a fine gentleman and prosperous business man, with new tailor made clothes, patent leather shoes and his favored silk tile, was rapid after he got his hands on the money I borrowed from the jewelers, with my diamonds as the pledge. The change in Swiftwater was simply marvelous. The day before almost, Swiftwater had stood before me, as I have told, without collar or tie, a dirty black growth of beard nearly an inch long on his unshaven chin and cheek, a dark frock coat of a nondescript shape that had seen better days and hung on Bill's frame as though it might have been loaned to him by some friend; a pair of trousers of mediocre workmanship and his feet almost sticking out of his shoes.

Then picture Swiftwater ready to board the steamer for San Francisco, where his friend Marks was waiting to grubstake him to the tune of $18,000, jauntily wearing his polished beaver on the side of his head, his black moustaches curled and waving in the breezes, his chin as smooth and immaculate as an ivory billiard ball and his air and manner that of a man who had absolute confidence in himself and his future.

It is no wonder then, that when Swiftwater reached San Francisco outfitted as I have described, he found plenty of men, who, charmed by the magic of his description of the golden lure of the North and hypnotized into a state of enthusiasm by the halo of romance and river beds lined with gold attached to Swiftwater's name, were willing to back him heavily for another venture in the North.

By this time the Tanana District was becoming famous throughout the world and the town of Fairbanks had been located and Cleary had brought forth from the stream that bears his name thousands of dollars of virgin gold, thus proving beyond question the richness of the country.

Now, I am ready to believe that most people will agree with me that Swiftwater was about as rapid and agile a performer as any of his contemporaries who occupy the hall of fame in the annals of Alaska. Because it was only a few short weeks until Swiftwater returns to Seattle with his pockets bulging with currency and prepared to leave for Fairbanks.

Of course, I knew nothing of Swiftwater's presence in Seattle, though it had been only a few short weeks since I had, with my own hands, in the kitchen in the little two-room apartment we occupied, washed his only suit of underclothes, so that he could go on the street without being annoyed by the police.

The first I knew of Swiftwater's return from San Francisco was when I read in the morning paper that "W. C. Gates, the well known and opulent Alaska miner," had entertained a distinguished party of Seattle business men at a banquet at one of the big down town hotels. The cost of that feed,

as I afterwards learned, was about $100—of Mr.
Marks' money. Be that as it may, before I could
find Swiftwater and gently recall to him the fact
that his wife and two little children were almost
in absolute want in Seattle he had managed to
board a steamer for the Tanana and was off for the
North.

Now, when I found that Swiftwater had gone, I
was frantic with the desire to follow him up to
Alaska. For the year and a half that I had remained
in Seattle, waiting like Micawber for something to
turn up, the fever to get back to Alaska seemed to
be growing in my veins at a rate that meant that
something had to be done. For, after Alaska has
once laid her spell over a man or woman, in nine
times out of ten, she will claim him or her from
that time onward to the end of life as her devoted
and always loyal slave. I know not, nor have I
ever found any who did know, what it is that
makes one who has ever lived in Alaska, and
who has left there, unhappy and discontented until
they go back once more to the land of gold.

I have seen and talked with old "sourdoughs,"
trappers and dog team freighters, and they all tell
the same story. When the first big cleanup had
been made in Dawson, I remember well, the winter
following found a mob of big, boisterous, pleasure
loving, money spending, carefree and happy hearted

Klondike miners in the hotels of Seattle, San Francisco and New York. They lived on nothing but
the choicest steaks and the richest wines, and the
sight of a plate of beans would start a fight. Then
they would all come back to Seattle in the spring,
sick, feverish, unhappy, with a look in their eyes
like that of a mother hungering for her lost babe.
In Seattle they would spend a restless week, but
when they struck the trail at White Horse just
before the spring breakup in the Yukon every man
jack of them was himself again—jolly, joyous, carefree, full voiced and filled with the enthusiasm of
a two-year-old.

Why, I have known more than one broad shoul-
dered giant of the trail grow as sick and puny as a
singed kitten while waiting in Seattle for his boat
to take him, late in February or early in March, to
Skagway. I knew one miner, who in health was
six feet five inches tall, weighing two hundred and
forty pounds without an ounce of fat on him, come
within an ace of dying with quick consumption,
which it afterwards proved was due to his longing
for the biting wind that blows from the top of
Alaska's Coast Range and bears company with the
wayfarer down in the valley of the Yukon past the
lakes and into the gold camps of the Klondike.

Well, all this came to me then as I realized that
Swiftwater was gone North once more in search

of gold, but, with Bera in Seattle and the two babies, I was shackled as securely as any one of the wretches who walk the streets of this city with chains and ball working out a sentence for vagrancy.

It is not a less remarkable thing to be told of Swiftwater that he turned Dame Fortune's wheel once more with the dial pointing in his direction as quickly as he had raised the necessary money in San Francisco to make a new start in Fairbanks. To all who know of Swiftwater's kaleidoscopic changes from rich to poor, and back again to rich, it seems as if the fickle Dame, carrying a magic horn spilling gold in all directions, followed Swiftwater wherever he went into Alaska and out again, down to the cities of the States and back again, and, if she seemed to lose him for a while, always to welcome him back with a winning smile.

Of course, it is part of my story that after Swiftwater had amassed another fortune on Cleary Creek, in the Tanana, and his friend, Mr. Marks, who had grubstake him, sought to obtain his rights in the property, it was found that the contract between them written by Swiftwater was as full of holes as a sieve. Again the lawyers went to work earning big fees in the litigation which Marks brought to compel Swiftwater to do the honorable thing—to do that by him which any man in Alaska, at least while he lived there, never failed to do—to divide with the man who grubstaked him.

Now, Swiftwater, as my reader has by this time safely guessed, was made in a different mould. They used to say in the early days when the stories of the incredible richness of Eldorado's gold lined bedrock were told on the "outside," that when a man in Alaska drank the water of the country, the truth left him. I have never, for my own part, fully determined whether this is true, and I may frankly say that in some of my experiences, the opportunities for judging of the truth or falsity of this theory were limited, the reason being that most of the men drink something beside water in that country.

As for Swiftwater Bill, he never did drink anything but water—I never knew him to take a drop of any intoxicating liquors or wine—so that if the water of Alaska had any demoralizing effect on Swiftwater, it must have been in the direction of his sense of business honor and integrity and a decent sense of his obligations as a husband and a father. And I am satisfied, too, that the water of Alaska, if such was the demoralizing agent in Swiftwater's case, certainly worked terrific havoc.

SWIFTWATER BILL GATES, FREDDIE GATES AT RIGHT,
AND CLIFFORD GATES, AT BOTTOM.

CHAPTER XIV.

SWIFTWATER BILL had struck it again.

On Number 6 Cleary Creek, in the Tanana, the man who gained his chiefest fame in the early days of Dawson by walking around the rapids of Miles Canyon, because he was afraid to navigate them, thereby earning his cognomen, "Swiftwater Bill," had found another fortune in the yellow gold that lines countless tens of thousands of little creeks and dry gulches in that great northern country—Alaska.

Swiftwater had obtained a big working interest in the mine on Cleary Creek, a stream that has produced its millions in yellow gold. And, after the first discovery of placer gold in paying quantities in the Tanana, the whole Western coast of the American continent knew the story. Like Dawson, the town of Fairbanks quickly sprang from the soil as if reared by the magic of some unseen genii of the Arabian Nights.

Of course, the word came out to me in a letter from a friend at Fairbanks. And I sometimes think that, after all, I must have had a great many friends in Alaska who remembered the hard task that the fates had put upon me when they made me, through no wish of my own, the mother-in-law of Swiftwater Bill.

As I remember now, the news that Swiftwater had struck another pay streak impressed upon me the necessity of immediate action. Swiftwater's previous conduct, particularly that $100 dinner that he gave in Seattle a few months before, had taught me one thing, and that was that if Gates was ever to do the square thing by me and by Bera and the babies it would be only when some one with sufficient will power to accomplish the task would reach him and see that he did not forget his duty.

Now, it is no May day holiday for a woman to "mush" over the ice from the coast of Alaska to the interior mining camps. First you have to get an outfit in Seattle, and by that I mean sufficient heavy underclothing, outer clothing, heavy boots, furs and sleeping bag and the like to make travel over the ice comfortable. Ten years ago any woman who made that journey—that is, from Dyea over the mountain passes covered with glaciers and thence down the Upper Yukon on the ice—was considered almost as a heroine and the newspapers were eager to print the stories of such exploits. When I determined to go into the Tanana to find Swiftwater mining gold on Number 6 Cleary there were few, if any, of the comforts of present-day winter travel

on the Valdez-Fairbanks trail, such as horse stages
and frequent road-houses.

Consequently, I determined to follow the old
route, and I went to Skagway, thence over the White
Pass road to White Horse and, crossing Lake Le-
Barge on the ice, there to await the departure for
Dawson of the first down river steamer.

It was in the early spring of the year—that is,
early for Alaska, although when I left Seattle the
orchards were in bloom and lawns were as green
as in mid-summer. Lake Le Barge was still frozen
over, and the upper waters of the Yukon
were beginning to show their first gigantic
unrest of that spring—a mighty unrest that carries
with it the movement of vast ice gorges down the
canyon of the Upper Yukon to the Klondike, and
which, if suddenly halted on its way to the sea by
an unexpected drop in temperature, is likely to work
havoc with men and property and sometimes human
lives.

The Yukon River is not like any other stream
on the American continent with which you and I are
familiar. It seems to be a thing alive when the
spring sun begins to loosen the icy chains that bind
it hard and fast to old Mother Earth through eight
long and dreary winter months. No greater phe-
nomena of nature, showing the change that spring
brings to all forms of life—human, animal and plant

—is to be found anywhere than the awakening of the Yukon River after her voiceless sleep.

At White Horse the freight for Dawson and the Tanana mines was stacked twenty feet high in all directions when we boarded the first steamer and followed the ice jam down the river to Dawson. Eventually, on a little steamer that plied between Dawson and Fairbanks when the ice is far enough gone to make navigation safe, I made my way to the chief mining camp of the Tanana—Fairbanks, named after the vice-president, who visited the North when he was a senator from Indiana.

I had no trouble in finding Gates.

"Swiftwater," I said, "I am here to have you provide for your wife and children, and to pay at least part of what you owe me."

Bill was courteous, suave, obliging and well mannered.

"Mrs. Beebe," said Bill, "at last I am fixed so that I can do the right thing by you and all others. As soon as I can make my last payment on my Cleary Creek property, I will square everything up, and give you plenty of money for Bera and the boys."

Now, I know that everyone who reads this little book will say to themselves:

"If Mrs. Beebe don't get her money now, she certainly is foolish."

Swiftwater, to be sure, saw that my hotel bills were paid and told me every day that in a short time he would clean up enough gold to make himself independent, and provide bountifully for Bera and the two boys—and I believed him.

Swiftwater's sister, the mother of Kitty, his polygamous wife, was, I quickly learned, living in a tent on Bill's claim, waiting to lay hold of him and his money as soon as the clean-up was finished. Long before this he had deserted Kitty, and in all the turmoil and trouble that came after his bigamous marriage to his niece I had lost all track of that unfortunate girl.

I remember now how odd it struck me that Swiftwater's sister was there, living in a little white canvas tent, and enduring the privations which any woman must suffer in that country, while I, actuated by the same desire, was waiting for Swiftwater to finish washing up the dumps on his claims. And I recalled at the time that when Swiftwater mined thousands of gold from his claims in the Klondike he allowed his own mother to cook in a cabin of a miner on a claim not far from his own, and although rich beyond his fondest dreams had permitted that poor woman to earn her own living by the hardest kind of drudgery and toil.

CHAPTER XV.

WIFTWATER'S cleanup on Number 6 Cleary Creek was $75,000 in gold. The summer was come to an end and there were signs on the trees, in the crackling of the frosted grass in the early morning and in the bite of the night wind from the mountain canyons that told of the quick approach of winter in the Tanana. Swiftwater had been more than usually fortunate. His mine on Number 6 Cleary had yielded far beyond his expectations. Swiftwater had every reason to believe his friends who told him that his luck was phenomenal.

As there are compensating advantages and disadvantages in almost every phase of human life in this world, it may possibly be said that as an offset to Swiftwater's phenomenal luck, he had two women, the mothers of his two wives, waiting patiently at Fairbanks for him to bring out enough money to properly provide for his families. I had told Swiftwater:

"I am up here to take good care of you, Bill, and incidentally to see that you provide enough money to feed and clothe your children and your wife. I don't care anything about that other woman over there.''

Bill laughed, and said it was probably a lucky thing for him that he had a mother-in-law to look after his welfare. But if Swiftwater's mind ever hovered around the idea of criminal proceedings on the score of bigamy, he did not give voice to it. He merely went around in his cheerful way from day to day working vigorously with his men until, finally, early in September, the last of the pay dirt was washed from the dumps into the sluice boxes and the gold sacked and taken to the bank.

Then Bill began paying off his debts. He settled with his partners, and then with a big chunk of bills and drafts in his inside pocket we started for Seattle.

It was getting winter rapidly and we had no time to lose in order to catch the steamship ''Ohio,' at St. Michael, for Seattle, before the winter freeze-up on Bering Sea.

Swiftwater, while working on Number 6 Cleary, had been all business and activity. Now, he seemed on the little boat going down the Tanana to be his old self again—by that I mean that Swiftwater reverted to his conduct of early days, which had lead some people to believe that he was descended from the Mormon stock back in Utah. Why Swiftwater had never earned the title of the Brigham Young of

the Klondike instead of the Knight of the Golden
Omelette or just plain Swiftwater, I never could
quite understand.

At Fairbanks Swiftwater induced a woman, whose
name I shall not give at this time, to board the
steamer for the outside. A half day's further ride
took us to Chena, and there Swiftwater met another
friend by the name of Violet—a girl who had worked
as housekeeper and cook for a crowd of miners during the summer because her husband had deserted
her and left her penniless in Fairbanks.

This Violet was young and comely, and of gentle
breeding. The hard life in the mining camps of
the Yukon and the bitterness she had suffered at
the hands of her truant husband had taken a little
of the natural refinement from the girl and had
probably shaped her life so that the better side could
not be seen.

Be that as it may, Violet came with Swiftwater,
but, when she found on the steamship "Ohio" that
Swiftwater had tipped one of the crew $100 so as
to enable him to have a seat with a woman on each
side of him at his meals, Violet refused to have
anything to do with him.

At St. Michael, when I found that Swiftwater
thought more of the association of women and of
having his kind of a good time than of providing for
his wife and children, I made up my mind that there

would have to be a showdown of some kind. I telegraphed to Bera at Seattle:

"Swiftwater is coming down on the Ohio. You had better see him now, if you want anything."

We were nine days making the trip from St. Michael to Seattle. When the crowd on the boat learned that Swiftwater Bill was on board, everybody looked for fireworks and a good time. The captain ordered notice put up in the dining room, reading:

"Gambling positively prohibited on this boat."

Swiftwater saw that sign and gently laughed to himself.

"Mrs. Beebe," he said, "I am going to have some fun with the boys. So if I come to borrow some money from you, don't be foolish and refuse me."

Swiftwater had some few hundred in cash, but most of his money was in drafts, which he could not cash on the boat. When I found that the boys had started a little poker game, I expected Swiftwater to be coming to me for money in a little while, and sure enough he did.

"Swiftwater," I said, "as long as you play poker you can't have any money from me, because you know you can't play poker. But if you will start a solo game I will let you have a little change."

Now, Swiftwater swelled up visibly because he

knew that I thought he was one of the best solo players in all the North, and I have to laugh even now to recall that after the first fifteen minutes of play at solo the men who had sought to fleece him of his money, found they had no chance and they all stopped the game.

It was late Saturday afternoon when finally the Ohio poked her nose in front of one of the docks in Seattle. There was a strong ebb tide, and it was nearly an hour before the gang plank was run ashore. We docked jam up against a little steamer on our left, and Swiftwater, being in a hurry to get ashore, asked me if I would take his grip in the carriage to the Cecil Hotel and he would join me in a little while, after he could get a shave. With that Swiftwater jumped to the deck of the little steamer next to us and thence to the dock and was gone.

I went direct to the Cecil Hotel, where Bera was waiting for me. Before I had been there a half hour the newsboys on the streets were crying the sale of the Seattle Times:

"All about Swiftwater Bill arrested for bigamy."

I heard the shrill voices of the urchins from my window in the hotel and I said:

"Bera, what have you done—had him arrested?"

I rang the bell and told the bell-boy to bring up a copy of The Times. Sure enough, there was the whole story of a warrant issued for Swiftwater Bill on the charge of bigamy and a long yarn about his various escapes in Alaska, including a recital of how he ruined the life of young Kitty Gates, his niece, by eloping with her and marrying her while he was still the lawful husband of Bera.

Just about dusk—I think it must have been at 8 o'clock that evening—there came a knock at the door. I went to answer it, and there in the hall of the hotel stood a man who was an absolute stranger to me.

"Mrs. Beebe?"

"This is Mrs. Beebe."

"Swiftwater wants to see you. I am Jack Watson, who used to be with him in the north."

"Where is he?" I asked.

"I can't tell you where he is, Mrs. Beebe," said the man, "but if you will go with me I can find him."

Five minutes later we were on First Avenue, which was crowded with thousands of sightseers, it being Saturday night, and everybody seemed to be out for a good time. Watson led me up Spring Street to the alley between First and Second Avenues and then went down the alley till, reaching the shadow of a tall building, he said:

"Please wait here a minute, Mrs. Beebe."

I looked down at the brilliantly lighted street cor-

ner on First Avenue, where is situated the Rainier-
Grand Hotel, and there I saw Swiftwater standing,
smoking a cigar, while hundreds of people were
passing up and down the sidewalk. He little
looked as if the deputy sheriffs were after him.

In a moment Watson had brought Swiftwater to
me.

"Mrs. Beebe," said Swiftwater, "what did you
wire to Bera? Did you tell her I was coming out
and to have me arrested?"

"I certainly wired her," said I, "and, Swiftwater, if she's had you arrested that's your business."

"Mrs. Beebe, you've been the only friend I've
ever had and now you have thrown me down," said
the miner.

Said I, "Swiftwater, I have not thrown you down,
and it's about time that you showed some indication
of trying to do what is right by me and Bera and
the babies."

"Here's that $250 I borrowed from you on the
boat," said Swiftwater, "and I guess after all that
you are really the only friend I ever had in this
world. Won't you tell me what to do now?"

I hesitated a moment and then it seemed to
me that there was little to be gained by having
Swiftwater thrown into jail without any chance
whatever to secure his release on bail. In spite

of all that I had suffered from him, and all the untold misery and humiliation that he had put upon my daughter Bera, I felt sorry for Swiftwater.

"You had better take this $250 back," said I, "as you may have to get out of town tonight. Have you any other money on you?"

"Not a cent," said he.

"Very well, you can pay me that money you owe some other time," I said.

Then Swiftwater and I fell to talking as to what had best be done. He wanted very much to see Bera and the babies and begged me, if I thought it safe, to take him to the hotel. Finally, seeing the big crowd on the streets, I consented, and together we went to the Cecil, entered the elevator and then went directly to my rooms.

Bera was there with the boy Freddie—the youngest. Swiftwater kissed Bera and the baby, but Bera turned away and went into another room, the tears streaming down her face.

"Mrs. Beebe," said Swiftwater, "the penitentiary will be my fate unless this bigamy charge is withdrawn. You and Bera and the babies will lose if I go to state's prison, and that is where Kitty Gates will send me unless Bera will get a divorce."

Just then there came a loud rap at the door, and without waiting for either of us to speak the door was opened and in walked two deputy sheriffs. They immediately placed Swiftwater under arrest.

CHAPTER XVI.

S A VERACIOUS chronicler of the events, inexplicable and unbelievable as this story may appear, of the life and exploits of Swiftwater Bill Gates, I want to begin this chapter with the prefatory announcement that, all and singular, as the lawyers say, the statements herein are absolutely true and may be verified.

I give this simple warning merely because, as I recall what happened the next two or three days after Swiftwater's arrest, it seems to me that many of my readers will say, "These things could not have. happened."

Swiftwater, calmly seating himself, in a big leather upholstered Morris chair, said, looking at the Sheriff; "Old man, I guess we can fix this thing up right here. Send for the judge and have him come down here quick."

The officer looked at me and smiled.

"I don't want to see Mr. Gates put in jail to-night" said I. "And if there is any way that this thing can be settled I am willing. More than that," and here I looked at Swiftwater, "I think Bill will not make any attempt to escape, and if it is all right with you, I'll go on his bond."

After more palaver of this kind, and here I am about to tell something about judicial processes that will surely cause a smile, a messenger was sent from the hotel to another hotel, where was stopping Judge Hatch, who was sitting on the Superior Court bench in King County, although he lived in another county down the Sound.

Outside in the hall there were a score of people, waiting to see Swiftwater, and to learn what would be the outcome of the case. There was the sheriff, Lou Smith; two other deputies, a half dozen lawyers and the reporters for the Seattle newspapers—quite a colony altogether.

After half an hour the judge came in the room, accompanied by another deputy sheriff.

"We'd just as well have some of the lawyers in here," said Swiftwater. "Ask Mr. Murphy and Mr. Cole to come in."

The door was opened and in came the attorneys and some others.

"Will you please ring the bell, Mrs. Beebe?" said Swiftwater.

I rang the bell, the boy came and Swiftwater ordered two pint bottles of wine.

Now, this was Swiftwater's way of dallying with justice. It was another exemplification of his idea —the mainspring in the man's whole character— that money could do anything and everything.

The wine came, two bottles at a time and then four, and then six. Every time the boy came up, Swiftwater borrowed money from me to pay the bill. Then Swiftwater did something that I never believed could happen. The National Bank at Fairbanks had, a few weeks before, issued its first currency—the first government bank notes in all Alaska. Swiftwater had a bunch of the new $20 bills and, wrapping in each a nugget taken from Number 6 Cleary, he presented one to each of his friends—that is, all who were present.

"If Mr. Gates will deposit $2,250, as counsel for Mrs. Gates desires, which is to be applied for the maintenance of herself and children and for attorney's fees, I think we may continue this matter until a later date," said the judge.

Swiftwater came over to me.

"I've got a thousand dollar draft," said he, "and if you will loan me $1,250 I'll pay everything up Monday," said Swiftwater.

I have never yet fully made up my mind what led me to loan Swiftwater that money, unless it was that, like everyone else who knew of his wonderful capacity for getting money rapidly out of the North, I believed he would make good all of his promises. I gave him the money, and Swiftwater was a free man.

Just then the sheriff himself opened the door and,

noticing one of the lawyers holding a bunch of bills and drafts in his hand, said:

"I guess I will take charge of this."

And so it came about that the money was deposited in the clerk's office in the county court, and on Monday morning, before any of us were about, the lawyers for Bera, Murphy & Cole, appeared in the courthouse with an order signed by the judge to draw the money out. Bera got $750 of the $1,000 promised her for maintenance for herself and children and the lawyers got the remainder.

Is it any wonder, then, that I have often thought it was the easiest thing in the world for Swiftwater to find a loophole in the meshes of the law by which he could escape, while I have never yet found a way to make the law give me just common justice?

And now it was Swiftwater's turn to act. In another day the newspapers had his story that he had been "held up," and after that came a sensation in the Bar Association of Seattle the like of which is not on record. And while the lawyers were fighting over the spoils, Swiftwater cleverly enough, though haunted by the spectre of the state prison, and constantly pressed by Kitty Gates, his polygamous wife, began working on Bera's sympathies. He came to the hotel and went to Bera's room.

"Bera," he said, "unless you get a divorce from me, and do it at once, Kitty will send me to the penitentiary; I will lose all my property in Alaska, and the boys and you will be everlastingly disgraced.''

Bera listened. It is enough to say that with Swiftwater in the penitentiary, his mining interests in Alaska, which promised brighter than anything he had ever undertaken, and that means hundreds of thousands of dollars, all of Bera's chance and mine to ever get a new start in life would have been wasted.

Swiftwater daily said:

''Bera, you certainly love the boys enough to save them the disgrace of having a felon for a father.''

The argument was enough. Bera consented, and although, as I understand it, the law specifically prohibits a divorce where the parties agree in advance on the severance of the holy marriage tie, Swiftwater went away and Bera brought suit for divorce in the court of King County. And in time the decree was granted and is still of record in that county.

A week later Swiftwater, as I afterwards found out, joined Kitty Gates in Portland and the two went to San Francisco. Thus can be turned into the basest uses the legal processes of our courts and, strange as it may seem, Swiftwater, after Bera's divorce, legally married Kitty, then divorced her, and not later than two years afterwards he told the newspapers in San Francisco, that having divorced all his other wives, he was looking for a new one.

I want to ask now, is there no law to reach a monster of this kind? Are the laws so framed that men of Swiftwater's type can go at large throughout the country ruining the lives of young girls, and, followed by a halo of gold and the fame that quick fortune making brings, claiming and receiving the friendship of their fellow men?

CHAPTER XVII.

I AM getting to the end of my story, and as the finish draws near, it seems to me, that I have not quite done justice by Swiftwater Bill, in at least one respect—and that is the activity and agility the man displays when events over which he might have had control, had he been on the square, crowded him so closely, that like the proverbial flea, he had to hike. And in telling of Swiftwater's talent in this direction, I wish to be regarded as speaking as one without malice, but rather as admiring Swiftwater for trying, in so far as lay in his power, to make good his nickname of Swiftwater.

In San Francisco, after Swiftwater had obtained a divorce from Kitty, he immediately announced his intention of getting another wife. For Swiftwater knew that the prison gates which once had yawned in his face were now closed, and, better even than that, was the thought that I—his loving mother-in-law—would no longer be interested in his future.

It is undoubtedly true that in Swiftwater's menta' processes he regarded first, the hundreds of thousands of dollars in gold that lay in the pay streak on No. 6 Cleary, in the Tanana, and I can see Bill now in my mind's eye, facing an array of cut glass decanters, embroidered table cloths, potted plants, orchestra and all that goes with the swell cafes of San Francisco, eating his dinner and rubbing his hands with glee as he remembered how easily he had obtained a fortune from me, which he sunk on Quartz Creek in the Klondike, and then slid out of paying his debt to me.

The very next season found Swiftwater in the Tanana and this time, according to the best official records I could obtain, his clean-up was not less than $200,000. But I had not forgotten that Swiftwater had told me, first that Number 6 Cleary was a bigger proposition even than Quartz Creek, and that Gold Stream was one of the richest of all the undeveloped creeks in the whole Tanana.

For this last information, I will say, I have always been grateful to Swiftwater, because his belief that the time would come when Gold Stream would be one of the best producers in all Alaska, led me to obtain several claims there. And now, let it be known, his prediction has been fully and completely verified.

But, knowing nothing of Gold Stream, and remembering only that Swiftwater had added more than $1,000 to his already great obligations to me, and had provided nothing for his family, I journeyed once more across the Coast Range of Alaska.

Crossing on the railway from Skagway to White Horse, I met a score or more of traders with their outfits of provisions and fresh vegetables, all hurrying to get into Dawson as soon as the ice broke up, to sell their wares to the miners of the Klondike at fancy prices. There were several women in the party, some of them bent on joining their husbands in Dawson.

Three hours ride down the river on a scow, laden with freight of every character, we struck a sand bar and were compelled to spent the night in midstream, absolutely without even a crust of bread to eat, and heaven's blue our only canopy. The grounding of freight scows in the upper waters of the Yukon in the spring is a common experience, and in those days little care was taken to protect the passengers from suffering hardship and real danger. That night the icy winds blew from the mountain ranges sixty miles an hour, and we suffered severely, not having a mouthful of food since the morning before.

The captain of the scow, oblivious to his obligations to his passengers, had loaned the only small boat he had to a pair of miners the day before. We could do nothing until they returned. Finally, after we had been on the bar for more than twelve hours, the men came back with the boat and took us, two at a time, ashore.

Then, guided by traders, the women in the party were told to walk down the stream fifteen miles to where there was a camp. It was bitter cold and the trail was hard to walk. In the afternoon of the day following our shipwreck, we stopped and the men built a bonfire, while the poor women fell almost unconscious in front of it, completely exhausted for want of food, which we had not tasted for twenty-four hours.

Two of the traders went down to the river's bank and on the other side they espied a camp of a herder, beneath the shelter of an abandoned barracks. This was the only human habitation within miles. The traders procured a boat and took us women across the river. The herder had some bacon and some dry bread, which he cooked for us. Now, I want to say that never in my life have I ever eaten anything that tasted so good as that meal, consisting only of fried bacon strips placed with the gravy on top of two slices of cold dry bread, and a teacup of hot coffee to wash it down with.

That day the scow came down the river and again we boarded it and finally reached Lake Lebarge. The lake was still frozen over and we started to cross its thirty miles of icy surface with horses drawing sleds. The ice was getting rotten and four times in as many miles, to my constant terror, the horses broke through the ice, threatening every minute to drag me with them. Becoming weary of this,

I left the sled and hired a dog team and outfit to take me across the lake.

At Clark's road house, I remained a week and then boarded a scow and went through Thirty-Mile river to board the steamer Thistle for Dawson. Going down the river on a scow, one scow that was lashed to ours, struck a rock in midstream, a hole was knocked into our scow, which almost sunk. The bank of the river was lined with thousands of people camping or moving on towards the Klondike. These people came to our rescue and with ropes and small boats helped us off.

In Fairbanks once more, I found Swiftwater. I had telephoned him of my coming, and in a day or two he came to my hotel.

"Mrs. Beebe," he said, "here is $50 for your present hotel bills. I must go back to Cleary Creek at once, but I will be back again inside of a week, and then I will straighten everything up."

When Swiftwater told me that, I believed him— for the last time—for the next morning I found that he had left my room to board a train for Chena, on the Tanana, with a draft for $50,000 in his inside pocket, $10,000 more in cash and a ticket for Seattle.

Swiftwater undoubtedly believed, that being without money I would be compelled to remain an unlimited time in Fairbanks. Not so. I still had a little jewelry left that he had not persuaded me to pawn or sell for his benefit, and on this I raised enough money to buy a ticket to Seattle.

Before I could get there, Swiftwater learned of my coming, and when I arrived on Elliott Bay, he had applied to the Federal Courts to be adjudged a bankrupt and had assigned to Phil Wilson all his interests in the Tanana, amounting to untold wealth.

That case of Swiftwater's is still pending in the Federal Court in Seattle, and no judge and no court has ever yet, up to this writing, consented to declare him a bankrupt, although he has successfully placed his property in the Tanana beyond the reach of the scores of men who have befriended him in the past without reward on his part.

CHAPTER XVIII.

GAIN it is spring, and I sit all alone in my room in Seattle, knowing that the city is filled with miners, their faces set in the direction of the Golden North, their hearts beating with high hopes, their breasts swelling with the happy purpose of getting back once more to the glacier bound, gold lined gravel beds of Alaska—the treasure land of the world. I know that I cannot go with them, for Swiftwater has robbed me of almost every farthing I ever possessed.

I read in the Seattle papers that scores of the old-timers are in the hotels down town, laying up stores of supplies, mining outfits, etc., ready for a big summer's season of work in the north, of digging far below the surface to the eternally frozen bedrock, in search of the only thing which is imperishable among all the perishable things of this earth—GOLD. I can see them thronging the hotel lobbies, the bars, and the cafes—great, burly, broad-shouldered, big-chested men of the North—the bone and sinew of the greatest gold-producing country in the world.

Many have bought their tickets and state-room reservations for the first Nome steamers, weeks in advance, unmindful of the fact that their ship must plough her dangerous way through great icebergs and ice floes in Bering Sea. Scores of others are planning to take the first boats of the spring season, while yet winter lingers with heavy hand on Alaska's coast and inland valleys, on their way to Valdez and thence over the ice to the Tanana, four hundred miles away. No thought of cold, or hardship, or danger deters any of these men, and even women, because they know at the end of the journey their mission will not be valueless, and that for at least a great proportion of them there will be a real shining pot of gold at the end of their rainbow of hope— where'er they find it—even though they must needs go as far as the rim of the Arctic Circle.

Many of my friends tell me that Swiftwater's life story, as I have set it down here, recounting only the facts, sparing nothing, adding nothing, will be eagerly read by tens of thousands of Alaska people. If this is true, then will Swiftwater be known in his true light to all that multitude of adventurous men and women of the North, who come and go through Seattle, fall and spring, spring and fall, like the myriads of Alaska's water fowl who seek the sunny South in October, to speed their way north again in the spring, the moment the ice floes in the headwaters of the Yukon are gone.

And now, as I survey my work, I am moved to ask all who read, if they can answer this question:

"What manner of man, in Heaven's name, is this Swiftwater Bill Gates?"

Yes, what manner of man, or other creature is Swiftwater? Perhaps some people will say that when Swiftwater Bill, down deep in his prospect hole on Eldorado, looked upon the glittering drift of gold that covered the bedrock, the glamor of that shining mass gave him a sort of moral blindness, from which he has never recovered. It is possible that the lure of gold, which he had seen in such boundless quantities, had so entered into his very soul that all sense of his duty and obligations as a man may have been dwarfed or utterly eliminated.

Be that as it may, Swiftwater, after he had placed his properties on Cleary Creek in the hands of Phil Wilson, so that his creditors could not lay hands on any of his money or by any means satisfy their just debts, went down into Nevada and plunged heavily in Rawhide and Goldfield properties. Rumors reached me many times that Swiftwater has made another fortune, and the San Francisco papers printed such stories about him. His property on Number 6 Cleary is still a big producer of gold, and it seems that by merely turning his hands, Swiftwater could, within a few months, pile up enough money to make happy those who have innocently suffered such grievous wrong at his hands. And here my heart grows hard as I think of the farce of the law—how fine are its meshes if an innocent person is taken—how wide are its loop holes when the smooth and oily crook with money becomes entangled therein.

For why is it, that the courts will suffer a lecherous monster to go abroad in the land, to marry and re-marry without paying the slightest heed to the restrictions of the law; to abduct, seduce and then abandon young girls and leave them penniless and deserted in unknown lands?

And, why is it that such men can, by using heavy tips of gold, weigh down the hands of the sworn officers of the law, manage to slip unharmed and unhampered through counties and states where the processes in bankruptcy and in criminal proceeding, issued by the courts of law, are out against them?

Why is it, then, that a man like Swiftwater could come to Seattle at night locked in the drawing room of a Pullman car, be taken swiftly in a closed carriage to a steamer bound for Valdez, and remain hidden in his stateroom on board the boat for two days before the ship sailed, while deputy sheriffs were scouring the town to compel him to provide from the ample money he had, food and clothing for the wife and babies he had deserted?

Perhaps, after all, Swiftwater's belief that the power of gold is omnipotent, may be the true and right one. Gold in the hands of such a man is a monstrous implement of crime, of degeneration to women and to innocent children.

CHAPTER XIX.

"AMA," don't you think you can have some fireworks on the Fourth of July and come out to the Brothers School so that we can celebrate?"

Little Freddie Gates, Swiftwater's youngest boy, looked up in my face with the dearest kind of a smile, and put his arm on my shoulder. The little fellow had just had his night bath in my room and had put on his fresh, clean, white pajamas, ready for bed.

It was Saturday before the Fourth of July and Freddie knew that I might not be able to spend Sunday with him at the Brothers School—which was the first Sunday since Freddie was taken there that I had not spent the day with him.

Now, it may seem odd to you and all the rest, who have followed the story of Swiftwater's fortunes and misfortunes, that I have never told you about the two dear little boys—Bera's children—who all these years have been without a father's care and who call their Grandma "Mama."

And this brings me to the story of how Clifford, the child who first saw the light of day on Gold Quartz Creek in order to satisfy his father's pride, as I have already told, was stolen from me by Lena Hubbell, the nurse. Clifford is the oldest boy of the two, and as dear a little fellow and as manly and straightforward and handsome as any boy you ever saw in your life. When the papers in Seattle told of Swiftwater making a big strike in the Tanana, Bera and I and all of us felt that at last there would be a brighter dawning and a better day, and an end of the drudgery and sacrifice and slavish toil which had been our portion.

A day or two after the story of Swiftwater's gold find came over the wires, Lena, into whose custody I had placed Clifford, came to me saying:

"Mrs. Beebe, if you don't care, I'd like to take Clifford on a little trip of two or three weeks to Mt. Vernon. I have some friends there and I need a vacation and a rest."

I had befriended Lena in the North and had done everything I could for her. I trusted the girl implicitly and it is not to be wondered at that I quickly gave her permission to take Clifford with her to Mt. Vernon, which is only a half day's ride or less from Seattle.

I told Lena to take good care of the child and be sure that she wrote me every few days—and this she promised to do.

Two weeks went by and I heard no word from Lena. I feared the child might be ill and wrote and then telegraphed without receiving an answer

to either. The last letter was returned to me un-
opened.

That afternoon I took the last train for Mt. Vernon, and before I went to bed in the little hotel there,
I found that my worst fears were true—Lena had
left, leaving no address, and had taken Clifford with
her. Later, I found she had taken the boy to Canada.

I have not heard directly from Lena and Clifford,
although I know what fate has befallen the boy,
and that he is alive and well. Of course, I do not
know that Lena Hubbell deliberately planned to
kidnap Clifford, believing that his father, when he
had amassed another fortune, would pay a large sum
for his recovery.

As soon as I had found in Fairbanks that Swiftwater was coming out, I urged him then and there,
with all the power and earnestness at my command.
to send an officer for Lena Hubbell and the child
into Canada and bring the boy home.

Swiftwater has not spent a dollar in this endeavor,
although it has cost me several hundred dollars in
futile efforts to bring the boy home.

Those two boys—Clifford and Freddie—are all
that I have left in this world to live for. Freddie
is seven years old, bright, plump, well developed
and very affectionate. It is said of him that he
learns very quickly and remembers well, and the

dear Fathers at the Brothers School at South Park, who have taken care of him, fed him and clothed him for months without a dollar of Swiftwater's money, say that he will some day make a name in the world.

And now, I am going to take you, my reader, into my confidence and tell you something that is sacred. These boys, I feel, are my own flesh and blood—my own boys.

If my story will throw some new light on the hardships of women who are forced to go to the North in search of a livelihood or shall be read with interest by all my old friends in Alaska, I shall rest content. I have a mission to perform—the care and education of my two boys—Clifford and Freddie.

THE END.

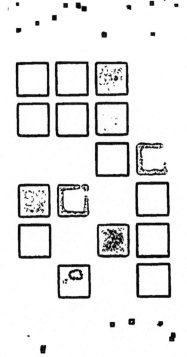

CPSIA information can be obtained
at www.ICGtesting.com
Printed in the USA
LVOW02*2348191216
518022LV00003B/72/P